OPEN ROAD'S BEST OF

Provence
& The French Riviera

by Andy Herbach

Open Road Publishing

Open Road's new travel guides.
Designed to cut to the chase.
You don't need a huge travel encyclopedia – you need a *selective guide* to steer you right. If you're going on vacation for a few weeks or less, get a guide that brings you the *best* of any destination for the amount of time you *really* have for your trip!

Open Road – the guide you need for the trip you want!

2nd Edition

OPEN ROAD PUBLISHING
P.O. Box 284, Cold Spring Harbor, NY 11724
www.openroadguides.com

Text Copyright © 2011 by Andy Herbach
- All Rights Reserved -

ISBN 10: 1-59360-123-9
ISBN 13: 978-1-59360-123-2
Library of Congress Control No. 2009924899

About the Author

Andy Herbach is a lawyer and resides in Milwaukee. He is the co-author of the *Eating & Drinking on the Open Road* series of menu translators and restaurant guides, including *Eating & Drinking in Paris*, *Eating & Drinking in Italy*, and *Eating & Drinking in Spain*. He is also the author of several Open Road guides, including *Open Road's Best of Paris* and *Open Road's Best of Spain*. You can e-mail him corrections, additions, and comments at eatndrink@aol.com. Updates can be found on the message board of his website: www.eatndrink.com.

Acknowledgments

French editor: Marie Fossier
English editors: Jonathan Stein and Marian Olson
Maps from designmaps.com
Contributor: Karl Raaum

For photo credits and acknowledgments, turn to page 215.

CONTENTS

Your Passport to the **Perfect Trip!**

12. PRACTICAL MATTERS   193

INDEX   207

Maps

1. INTRODUCTION

Some come to **Provence** for the savory cuisine and wonderful wines, while others visit quiet villages to get away from it all. There are also some of the world's best-preserved Roman ruins to see, and elegant seaside resorts where you can bask on sun-drenched beaches.

Whatever your reasons to visit, there's truly something for everyone in Provence and on the French Riviera.

You'll be dazzled by fields of lavender, yellow sunflowers and bright red poppies under brilliant blue skies. On the **French Riviera**, you'll discover pastel-colored villas with red tile roofs looking down on the turquoise waters of the Mediterranean Sea. Wherever you go, you'll create colorful memories.

You'll have over 100 places of interest at your fingertips (from the Papal Palace in Avignon to the wineries in Châteauneuf-du-Pape to colorful Old Nice), with insider tips on cafés, restaurants, hotels, shops, outdoor markets, and where to sample Provence's great wines. You'll visit the loveliest towns of Provence and the French Riviera, including Aix-en-Provence, Arles, Avignon, and Nîmes.

This guide covers all the information you need to plan your trip without burdening you with a long list of options that simply aren't worth your precious vacation time. Just take off and enjoy—you've got a great adventure ahead!

2. OVERVIEW

Get ready to explore Roman ruins, eat fantastic food, enjoy bustling outdoor markets, or just sit in the sun and sip a glass of chilled wine.

The Main Cities of Provence
Arles is one of the three "A's" that make up the most visited cities in Provence (along with Aix-en-Provence and Avignon). Arles has everything you could want in a Provence city: festivals, an Old Town, Roman ruins, cafés and intimate restaurants.

Aix-en-Provence is a graceful and sophisticated city. Between the

12th and 15th centuries it was the capital of Provence. Shaded squares with bubbling fountains in the Old Quarter, 17th-century town houses and the cours Mirabeau (the grand main avenue) make Aix a must for all visitors to Provence.

Although the last pope left in 1377, you're reminded of the papal legacy everywhere in modern-day **Avignon**. Its large student population makes it a vibrant city unlike most of the small villages of Provence.

Officially part of the Languedoc region, **Nîmes** is a popular destination for visitors to Provence. Some of the world's best-preserved Roman sights are here, giving it the nickname "the Rome of France."

Lovely Villages of Provence
There are so many lovely villages in Provence that it's hard to pick favorites. Depending on your interest, here are a few of my favorites and why I find them so appealing:

- **Saignon**: Quiet and Unspoiled
- **Lourmarin**: Fine Dining
- **Oppède-de-Vieux**: A Taste of Old Provence
- **L'Isle-sur-la-Sorge**: The "Venice of Provence"
- **Uzès**: An Overlooked Gem
- **Cassis**: Sun-Drenched Beaches

Marseille & the Coast

Cosmopolitan and diverse **Marseille**, the breathtaking Grand Canyon du Verdun, vineyards and seafront resorts offer the traveler a little bit of everything in this area of Provence.

The Western French Riviera: From St-Tropez to Nice

Hilltop villages, art museums, coastal resorts and a St-Tropez tan all await you in the western French Riviera.

Nice

Nice has on average 300 sunny days a year, many important historical sights and museums, a fabulous **Old Town**, and great dining.

Two Weeks in Provence & the Riviera

For your first week, spend a weekend in **Avignon** and then visit the towns of the **Luberon region**. For your second week, visit **Aix** and try to hit the towns in and around **Arles**. If you have two (or more) weeks in the **French Riviera**, I recommend that you base yourself in **Nice** for the first week and visit the area east of Nice toward the Italian border. For your second week, stay in **St-Tropez, Cannes** or **Antibes** and visit the area west of Nice. Or combine parts of Provence and parts of the Riviera and get the best of both!

The Eastern French Riviera: From Nice to the Italian Border

The French lifestyle with an Italian feel greets you in this part of the French Riviera.

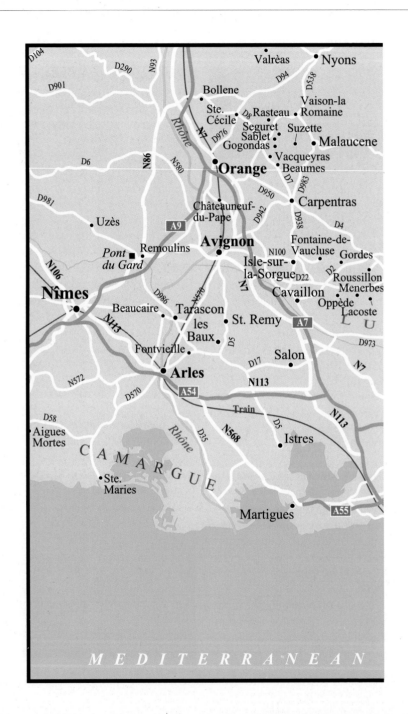

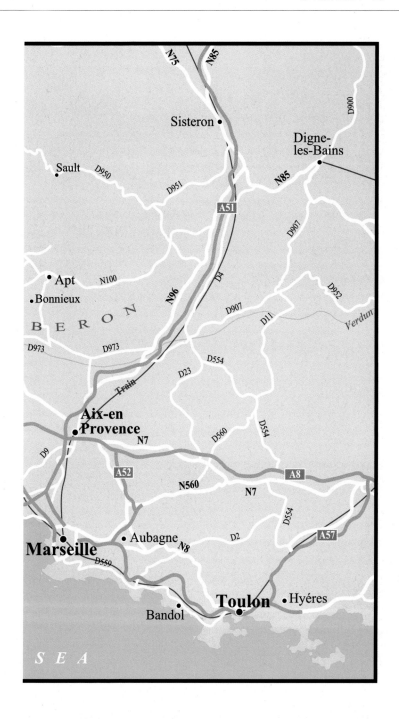

3. NORTHERN PROVENCE

HIGHLIGHTS

▲ Roman ruins, especially those at Nîmes and the Pont du Gard

▲ Unspoiled medieval villages like Séguret

▲ Beautiful wine country, centered around Châteauneuf-du-Pape

▲ Undiscovered gems like the village of Uzès

INTRO

Northern Provence is home to impressive Roman structures like the **Pont du Gard**, the ruins found in the fortified medieval village of **Vaison-la-Romaine,** the massive theatre of **Orange**, and

COORDINATES

Northern Provence is in the south of France. The largest city, **Nîmes**, has a population of 140,000. The towns are within 25 miles (40km) of Avignon and about 400 miles (644km) south of Paris.

some of the world's best-preserved Roman sights of **Nîmes**, "the Rome of France." After you've viewed the extraordinary Roman sights, you can slow down in the quaint medieval villages of **Séguret** and **Le Barroux** or head to undiscovered **Uzès**. Top it all off by drinking the delicious wines of the vineyards of **Châteauneuf-du-Pape!**

Note: Many attractions and offices in Provence close at noon and reopen an hour or two later.

SIGHTS

A WEEK IN NORTHERN PROVENCE

Vaison-la-Romaine
The fortified medieval village of **Vaison-la-Romaine** seems to hang precariously over the road as you approach. It's 20 miles (32 km) northeast of Avignon/17 miles (27 km) northeast of Orange. The village is divided into two by the Ouvèze River. The Roman bridge connects **Ville-Basse** (the Roman and present-day town) and **Ville-Haute** (the medieval town). A lively market fills **la place François-Cevert** every Tuesday morning and early afternoon.

Head to the **Roman Ruins** in the Ville-Basse. The ruins are split by a modern road (avenue Général-de-Gaulle). The **Quartier de Puyim** has remains of a 6,000-seat theatre, temples, courthouse (praetorium), and foundations of homes including the **Maison des Messii**. The **Musée Théo-Desplans**, an archeology museum, is here. Across the street is the **Quartier de la Villasse** with the remains of a Roman village, including its baths (and marble toilets). *Info: In Ville Basse (avenue Général-*

de-Gaulle). Open daily. Admission: €8 (includes admission to the cloister at Cathédral Notre-Dame-de-Nazareth, below).

Also worth a look is the **Cathédral Notre-Dame-de-Nazareth**. One of the finest examples of Provençal Romanesque architecture, this cathedral is known for its sculpted cloister. *Info: avenue Jules-Ferry. Open daily. Admission: €8 (includes admission to the Roman ruins, above).*

Now it's time to head to the **Haute Ville** (Upper Town).

From the Roman ruins on avenue Général-de-Gaulle toward the river, you'll cross the 2,000-year-old Roman bridge (**Pont Romain**). In the 1990s, a flood destroyed a nearby modern bridge, but left the Roman bridge intact! Explore the fortified medieval village high above the river valley. You'll pass 13th- and 14th-century homes on your way through a twisted maze of steep cobblestone streets. At the highest point are the ruins of a castle built in 1160 by the Count of Toulouse.

While in the Upper Town, you're going to get quite hungry climbing the steep streets. A good place to relax, eat and drink is at **Les Terrasses du Beffroi** on the garden terrace at the Beffroi Hotel. *Info: rue de l'Évêché (in the Upper Town). Tel. 04/90.36.04.71. Closed Mon and Nov-Mar. Moderate.*

Séguret & Le Barroux

We'll visit two medieval villages today: Séguret and Le Barroux.

The quaint medieval village of **Séguret** clings to the foothills of the Dentelles de Montmirail, a series of limestone rocks stretching skyward. It's five miles (nine km) southwest of Vaison-la-Ro-

SIGHTS

maine. You can climb its car-free and steep cobblestone streets lined with vine-covered stone homes. There are three medieval gateways, the 12th-century church **Eglise St-Denis**, a 15th-century fountain, and castle ruins. A truly lovely town. Take in the sweeping views of the vineyards on the plain below and don't leave this area without stopping at one (or a few) of them.

I recommend you unwind at **Le Mesclun**, a village restaurant serving Provençal dishes at reasonable prices. Great views of the surrounding vineyards from the outdoor terrace. *Info: rue des Poternes. Tel. 04/90.46.93.43. Open April-October. Moderate.*

If you thought Séguret was unspoiled, wait until you see **Le Barroux**! It's ten miles (16 km) south of Vaison-la-Romaine/21 miles (34 km) northeast of Avignon. A maze of narrow streets with ancient fountains makes this unspoiled hill town worth a visit. You can tour the restored vaulted rooms of the imposing fortified *château* and Renaissance chapel. The castle is a frequent site for contemporary-art exhibits. *Info: Tel. 04/90.62.35.21. Open daily Jun-Oct. Weekends only Apr-May. Admission: €5.*

Orange
Today we'll visit the magnificent Roman structures of **Orange**. It's 19 miles (31 km) north of Avignon/6 miles (10 km) north of Châteauneuf-du-Pape.

Orange's name dates back to when it was governed by the Dutch House of Orange. It became a thriving Roman city filled with public baths, temples, and monuments. In the 13th century, many of the Roman buildings were demolished and the stone used to build a defensive wall. Today most visitors come to this town overlooking the Rhône Val-

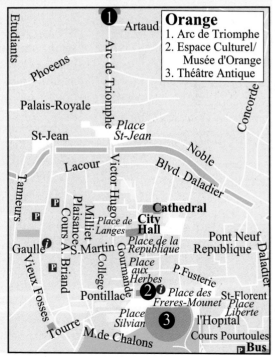

SIGHTS

ley to see two magnificent Roman structures that survived.

The massive Roman theatre (**Théâtre Antique**) was built in the time of Caesar Augustus, and his statue on the center stage still survives. This is the best-preserved Roman theatre in the world.

Its acoustic wall remains, and if you climb the stairs to the top of the semi-circle of theatre seats you can still hear conversations of those on the stage: a testament to the acoustical-engineering skills of its classical designers. Plays and musical events are still held here, and there's an opera and classical music fair, called **Les Chorégies d'Orange**, every July. An archeological dig of an ancient gymnasium is located adjacent to the theatre.

Also on the same square is the **Espace Culturel/Musée d'Orange**. This small museum displays Roman antiquities and has a gift shop. It's across the street from the Théâtre Antique. *Info: place des Frères-Mounet. www.theatre-antique.com. Tel. 04/90.51.17.60. Open Jan, Feb, Nov, and Dec 9:30am-4:30pm; Mar and Oct 9:30am-5:30pm; Apr, May and Sep 9am-6pm; Jun-Aug 9am-7pm. Admission: €8 (includes audio guide and entry to the Théâtre Antique, see above).*

Orange
1. Arc de Triomphe
2. Espace Culturel/ Musée d'Orange
3. Théâtre Antique

SIGHTS

If you're dining here, try **La Grotte d'Auguste** inside the Théâtre Antique. This unique restaurant serves Provençal fare in stone rooms and on the terrace with views of the Roman theatre. *Info: Théâtre Antique. Tel. 04/90.60.22.54. Open daily. Moderate.*

If you're really into Roman structures, check out the **Arc de Triomphe** north of the city center at the traffic circle on avenue Arc de Triomphe (in the direction of Gap). This incredibly well-preserved 60-foot-tall Roman arch was built between 49 and 20 B.C., and is decorated with battle scenes.

Châteauneuf-du-Pape

Get ready to drink some wine in **Châteauneuf-du-Pape**. It's 6 miles (10 km) south of Orange/14 miles (23 km) west of Carpentras/11 miles (18 km) north of Avignon.

This town's history is linked

Wine Tasting

You're in the heart of wine country. Look for signs saying **Cave Coopérative** at vineyards. If they say **dégustation**, this means free wine tastings are offered. Although there's no obligation to buy, you should get at least one bottle (especially if you've spent some time at the winery).

to the popes of Avignon. The *château* towering over the town was built by the popes in the 14th century as a summer residence, and was badly damaged by bombing during World War II. Vineyards, said to have been planted by the popes, surround the lovingly restored town whose names means "new castle of the pope." Today, the wines from this area are known the world over. In 1954 the village council passed an ordinance prohibiting the landing of flying saucers (they called them "flying cigars") in their vineyards. (This ordinance has worked well in discouraging such landings).

A wine festival (**Fête de la Véraison**) is held for three days in early August. Locals dress in medieval costumes, and area wineries set up stalls. For

Wine Words

wine, vin
wine list, carte des vins
red wine, vin rouge
rosé wine, vin rosé
white wine, vin blanc
bottle, bouteille
half-bottle, demi-bouteille
glass, verre
full-bodied, robuste

about €3, you purchase a souvenir glass and sample all the wine you want. If you start seeing wine coming out of the attractive fountain in the place du Portail, you're not that drunk; it really does spurt wine during the festival.

After exploring the town, head to route D17, and stop at the **Musée du Vin/Caves Brotte**. Located in the cellar (cave) of a family winery, this museum celebrates the area's wine making tradition. And yes, there are wine tastings. *Info: avenue le Bienheureux Pierre du Luxembourg (route D17). Tel. 04/ 90.83.70.07. Open daily. Admission: Free.*

There are over 20 area wineries where you can taste the wines of Châteauneuf-du-Pape. **Clos des Papes** is conveniently located on the route

to Avignon. *Info: 13 avenue le Bienheureux Pierre du Luxembourg (route D17). Tel. 04/ 90.83.70.13. Open daily.*

Pont du Gard

Today we'll view Roman ingenuity at the **Pont du Gard** *(see photo on page 17)*. It's 23 miles (37 km) southwest of Orange/13 miles (22 km) southwest of Avignon.

How did they do it? Two thousand years ago, the **Romans** built a system to carry water 30 miles from a spring near Uzès to Nîmes. The Pont du Gard is a huge three-tiered, arched aqueduct spanning the Gardon River. It's the second tallest Roman structure in the world. Only the Coliseum in

SIGHTS

Rome is taller. The aqueduct once carried 44 million gallons each day. The 80-foot main arch is the largest ever built by the Romans. When I first visited the aqueduct, you were able to walk on the very top (a scary and dangerous experience).

Today, the aqueduct is off-limits. Visitors flock here and marvel at the sheer size of this tribute to Roman ingenuity. A **museum** at the visitor center highlights the history of the aqueduct, and there's an informative film that plays every half hour. *Ludo* is an interactive kids' zone (in English). There's a café for light meals and a restaurant offering regional specialties. You can swim in the river below, dive off part of the aqueduct, or rent a canoe (which is a great way to experience the aqueduct). *Info: www.pontdugard. fr. Tel. 04/66.37.51.10. Open daily 9:30am-5:30pm (May-Sep until 7pm). Ludo closed Mon morning and part of Jan. Admission: Parking: €5. Museum: €7. Film: €4. Ludo: €5. A ticket for parking and the museums can be purchased for €12.*

Uzès

Don't bypass **Uzès** on the border of Provence in the Languedoc region. It's 15 miles (25 km) north of Nîmes/ 24 miles (39 km) west of Avignon. Begin your visit to this lovely town at the imposing **Cathédrale St-Théodorit** (you can't miss it, and there's a large car park next to it). The cathedral, built on the site of a Roman temple, dates back to 1652. Those are the remains of St-Firmin in the glass coffin on the left side of the cathedral. When outside, look up at the **Tour Fénestrelle**. Doesn't it look like the Leaning Tower of Pisa? As you face the cathedral, there's a former palace to your left

(**Palais Episcopal**) that now houses the city's courts of law.

Across the street from the cathedral is the Old Town where you'll find the **ducal palace** on place du Duché. Descendents of the House of Uzès still live here. *Info: Open daily. Admission: €12 (French-only tour).* But don't come here just for the palace, come to walk the beautiful and car-free Old Town, and to visit the **medieval garden** on rue Port Royal. *Info: Open daily, admission: €4.* The **place aux Herbes** with sheltered walkways and medieval homes is a relaxing place to take a coffee break, although it's not so calm on Wednesday mornings and Saturdays when it hosts a lively market.

Nîmes
Officially part of the Languedoc region, **Nîmes** is a

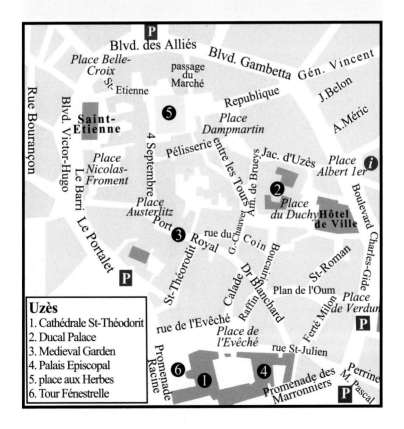

Uzès
1. Cathédrale St-Théodorit
2. Ducal Palace
3. Medieval Garden
4. Palais Episcopal
5. place aux Herbes
6. Tour Fénestrelle

SIGHTS

popular destination for visitors to Provence. It's 26 miles (43 km) southwest of Avignon/ 19 miles (31 km) northwest of Arles. Some of the world's best-preserved Roman sights are here, giving it the nickname "the Rome of France." The town is dotted with Roman ruins such as the **Tour Magne** (a tower on Mont Cavalier and the city's oldest monument). It's frenetic and not at all like the calm small villages of Provence. Did you know that denim (the material that all those jeans are made of) was created here in the Middle Ages? The Old Town is easily explored on foot, and is home to the major sights.

Begin your day at the tourist office at 6 rue Auguste where you can pick up a free map. It's near the first site that we'll visit today (you can't miss it).

The steel-and-glass **Carré d'Art** is home to a contemporary art museum featuring works created after 1960. You can stop for refreshments at the rooftop café here. It has a great view of the Roman temple and other landmarks. *Info: place de la Maison Carrée. Tel. 04/ 66.76.35.70. Open Tue-Sun*

10am-6pm. Closed Mon. Admission: €5.

Head across the street. Built around 5 B.C., the incredibly well-preserved **Maison Carrée** is a Roman temple modeled after the Temple of Apollo in Rome. It was the model for the Eglise de la Madeleine in Paris, the state capitol of Virginia, and many other buildings featuring Corinthian columns. The interior houses changing exhibits. *Info: place de la Comédie (boulevard Victor-Hugo). Tel. 04/66.21.82.56. Open daily. Admission: €5.*

As you leave the Roman temple, the street between it and the art museum is boulevard Victor Hugo. Head down the boulevard in the opposite direction of the tourist-information shop. You'll pass the place de la Madeleine (to your right on boulevard Victor Hugo). Soon you'll see a large arena.

Look familiar? The well-preserved arena (**Amphithéâtre Romain**) is a miniature of the Colosseum in Rome. It held over 20,000 people who watched gladiators fight. Today, it's used for performances and an occasional bullfight. In the 13th century, the arena was inhabited by nearly 700 people who created a miniature village inside. Napoleon changed all that when he designated it a historic monument. *Info: place de Arènes. Tel. 04/66.21.82.56. Open daily 9:30am-5pm (Jan, Feb, Nov, and Dec), 9am-6pm (Mar and Oct), 9am-6:30pm (Apr, May, and Sep), 9am-7pm (Jun), 9am-8pm (Jul and Aug). Admission: €8.*

Across the street from the arena is the **Musée des Cultures Taurines**, a bullfighting museum, at 6 rue Alexandre-Ducros. *Info: Tel. 04/66.36.83.77. Open Tue-Sun 10am-6pm. Closed Mon. Admission: €5.*

Other sights of interest here include the following three on boulevard de l'Amiral-Courbet:

The **Musée Archéologique et d'Histoire Naturelle**, a museum of archaeology and natural history, is filled with statues, friezes, pottery, and coins. *Info: 13 bis boulevard de l'Amiral-Courbet. Tel. 04/66.76.74.80. Open Tue-Sun 10am-6pm. Closed Mon. Admission: Free.*

The **Porte d'Auguste** is a gate built during the reign of Augustus. Across the street is the church **Eglise St-Baudile**, named after the martyr and patron saint of the city.

In the Old Town are two sights next to each other that are worth a visit.

The **Cathédral Notre-Dame et St-Castor** has a beautifully preserved Romanesque frieze

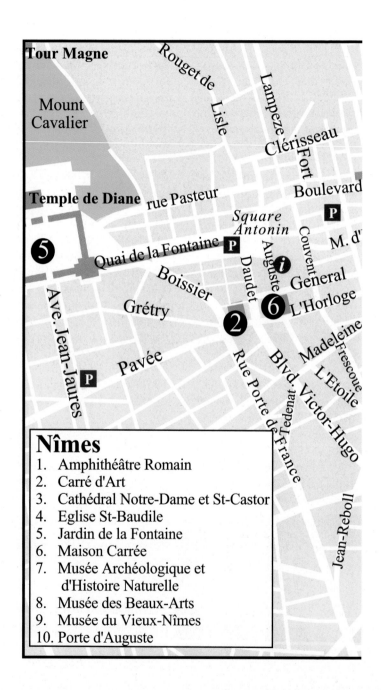

Tour Magne

Mount Cavalier

Rouget de Lisle

Lampeze

Clérisseau

Fort

Boulevard

Temple de Diane rue Pasteur

Square Antonin

M. d'

Quai de la Fontaine

Auguste

Couvent

Daudet

General

Boissier

Grétry

L'Horloge

Ave. Jean-Jaures

Madeleine

Frescoue

Pavée

Rue Porte de France

Blvd. Victor-Hugo

Tedenat

L'Etoile

Jean-Reboll

Nîmes

1. Amphithéâtre Romain
2. Carré d'Art
3. Cathédral Notre-Dame et St-Castor
4. Eglise St-Baudile
5. Jardin de la Fontaine
6. Maison Carrée
7. Musée Archéologique et d'Histoire Naturelle
8. Musée des Beaux-Arts
9. Musée du Vieux-Nîmes
10. Porte d'Auguste

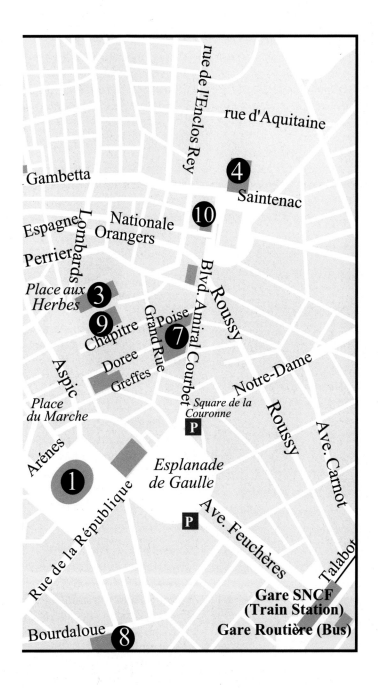

SIGHTS

featuring Adam, Eve, Abel, and Noah. Construction began on this cathedral in 1096. The inside features a 4th-century sarcophagus. *Info: place aux Herbes. Open daily. Admission: Free.*

Off of place aux Herbes (near the cathedral) is the **Musée du Vieux-Nîmes** (Museum of Old Nîmes) showcasing life in Nîmes in the Middles Ages, including a 14th-century jacket made of the famous *denim de Nîmes*, the fabric that Levi-Stauss used for blue jeans. *Info: Place aux Herbes. Tel. 04/66.76.73.70. Open Tue-Sun 10am-6pm. Closed Mon. Admission: Free.*

You need to take a break, as we've visited a lot of sights today. You'll find plenty of cafés at the lively **place de l'Horloge** (Clock Square).

After lunch, there are two other places of interest that you might want to check out.

The **Musée des Beaux-Arts** is the city's fine-arts museum. You'll find not only French paintings and sculpture, but also a large collection of Flemish and Italian paintings, including Ruben's *Portrait of a Monk*. A well-preserved Gallo-Roman mosaic is also here. *Info: rue de la Cité-Foulc. Tel. 04/66.67.38.21. Open Tue-Sun 10am-6pm. Closed Mon. Admission: €5.*

One of the most beautiful gardens in all of France is the **Jardin de la Fontaine** (*see photo at top left of next page*). Designed in the 18th century, the chestnut trees shade stat-

Top Roman Sights

- The **Pont du Gard**, a huge three-tiered, arched aqueduct spanning the Gardon River (13 miles southwest of Avignon)
- **La Trophée des Alpes**, towering over the village of La Turbie in the hills above Monaco
- The theater and arena in **Arles**
- The ruins and 2,000-year-old bridge (Pont Romain) in **Vaison-la-Romaine**
- The **Théâtre Antique** and **Arc de Triomphe** in Orange
- The ruins of a Gallo-Roman village (**Glanum/Les Antiques**) in St-Rémy
- The theatre, arena and aqueduct in **Fréjus**
- The Roman gate and tower in **Nîmes**

SIGHTS

Pétanque

What game are all those men playing in squares throughout Provence? **Pétanque**, also called *boules*, is played in every Provençal village. A *boule* is a metal ball the size of a baseball. The player who gets his *boule* closest to the target ball (*le cochonnet*) wins. Okay, this is a very simplified version of the game, but you get the picture: French lawn bowling, but it's played on sand!

ues, urns, and the remains of a Roman shrine. At the end of the garden are the ruins of the 1st-century **Temple de Diane**. A great way to end your day in Nîmes. *Info: End of quai de la Fontaine. Open daily. Admission: Free.*

SLEEPS & EATS

BEST SLEEPS & EATS

CHÂTEAUNEUF-DU-PAPE
Le Pistou €-€€
This restaurant takes its name from *pistou* (a sauce made of garlic, basil, nuts and olive oil), the Provençal version of Italian *pesto*. Several dishes feature *pistou*, such as the delicious *soup au pistou*. Local dishes at very reasonable prices. *Info: 15 rue Joseph-Ducos (near the Hôtel de Ville (City Hall)). Tel. 04/90.83.71.75. Closed Sun (dinner) and Mon and in Jan.*

LE BARROUX
Les Géraniums €
This family-owned, 22-room hotel in an unspoiled hill town also

has a great restaurant. Relax on the beautiful flowered terrace where meals are served. Try the *plateau de fromages de France*, a platter of delicious French cheeses. *Info: place de la Croix. www.hotel-lesgeraniums. Tel. 04/90.62.41.08. Closed in winter. V, MC. Restaurant (€-€€), telephone.*

ORANGE
Hôtel Arène €-€€
Four town houses have been combined to create this unique 35-room hotel in the historic Old Town. Traditional furnishings, a helpful staff and a quiet location on a pedestrian street all make this a good option while in Orange. *Info: Place de Langes. www.hotel-arene.fr. Tel. 04/90.11.40.40. V, MC, DC, AE. TV, telephone, minibar, hairdryer, safe.*

La Grotte d'Auguste €€
This unique restaurant, located inside the Théâtre Antique, serves Provençal fare in stone rooms and on the terrace with

views of the Roman theatre (*photo at right*). *Info: Théâtre Antique. Tel. 06/76.04.43.83. Open daily.*

NÎMES

Imperator Concorde €€-€€€

This recently renovated 60-room hotel is located near one of the most beautiful gardens in all of France, the Jardin de la Fontaine. Rooms are decorated with traditional regional furnishings, and the bathrooms are quite modern. The lovely restaurant ("L'Enclos de la Fontaine") serves local specialties,

and the Hemingway bar opens onto the peaceful garden. *Info: Quai de la Fontaine. www.hotel-imperator.com. Tel. 04/ 66.21.90.30. V, MC, DC, AE. Restaurant, bar, AC, TV, telephone, minibar, hairdryer, safe.*

Hôtel l'Amphithéâtre €

This 15-room hotel is the budget choice in Nîmes. Located in an 18th-century, formerly private home, it's crammed with antiques. You may feel a little cramped in the small rooms (with small bathrooms), but the price and location are right. *Info: 4 rue des Arènes. Tel. 04/66.67.28.51; hotel-amphitheatre@wanadoo.fr. V, MC. TV. Closed most of Jan.*

Chez Jacotte €€

On a narrow street in the Old Town, this lovely restaurant serves Provençal specialties. You can dine indoors under a vaulted ceiling, or outdoors overlooking a medieval square. *Info: 15 rue Fresque. Tel. 04/66.21.64.59. Closed Sat (lunch), Sun and Mon.*

Vintage Café €-€€

This popular wine bar in the Old Town serves local food at reasonable prices. Try the bull steak or *fois gras*. *Info: 7 rue de Bernis. Tel. 04/66.21.04.45. Closed Sat (lunch), Sun and Mon.*

SÉGURET

Le Mesclun €€

Village restaurant serving Provençal dishes at reasonable prices. Great views of the surrounding vineyards from the outdoor terrace. *Info: rue des Poternes. Tel. 04/90.46.93.43. Closed Mon.*

UZÈS

Hôtel du Général d'Entraigues €-€€

This 36-room hotel is housed in converted 17th- and 18th- century private homes near the cathedral. It has a lovely swimming pool

and a good restaurant, "Les Jardins de Castille," serving food on the terrace. *Info: 8 rue de la Calade (at place de l'Évêché). www.hoteldentraigues. com. Tel. 04/ 66.22.32.68. V, MC, AE. Restaurant, bar, outdoor pool, AC, TV, telephone, minibar, hairdryer, safe.*

Les Fontaines €€

Indoor and outdoor dining at this restaurant serving the cuisine of the Languedoc region in a 12th-century building in the center of Old Town. Try the flavorful *filet mignon de porc! Info: 6 rue Entre les Tours. Tel. 04/66.22.41.20. Open daily July and Aug. Closed Wed and Thu the rest of the year. Moderate.*

VAISON-LA-ROMAINE

Hôtel Beffroi €-€€

Located in a beautiful 16th-century mansion in the Upper Town, this 22-room, family-owned hotel offers panoramic views of the surrounding area. There's a garden terrace, an outdoor pool, and parking both at the hotel (a rarity in the Upper Town) and at the foot of the Upper Town. You'll need a break after climbing the steep streets of the medieval town. Try the hotel's restaurant in the garden terrace *Info: rue de l'Évêché (in the Upper Town). www.le-beffroi.com. Tel. 04/ 90.36.04.71. V, MC, DC, AE. TV, telephone, hairdryer. mini-bar. Closed Feb-Mar. Restaurant €€.*

BEST SHOPPING

Orange
Thursday-morning **food and flea market** on cours A.-Brians.

Uzès
The place aux Herbes hosts a lively **market** on Wednesday mornings and Saturdays.

Vaison-la-Romaine
A **market** fills place François-Cevert every Tuesday morning and early afternoon, and Sundays in July and August.

Châteauneuf-du-Pape
There are over 20 area wineries where you can taste the wines of Châteauneuf-du-Pape. **Clos des Papes** is conveniently located on the route to Avignon. *Info: avenue le Bienheureux Pierre du Luxembourg (route D17). Tel. 04/90.83.70.13. Open daily.*

NIGHTLIFE & ENTERTAINMENT

BEST NIGHTLIFE & ENTERTAINMENT

Northern Provence is not known for its nightlife. Your best bet is in **Nîmes**.

Nîmes
Head to the boulevard Victor-Hugo or the area around the place de la Maison Carrée. Among the lively cafés here are the **Café Le Napol éon** at 46 boulevard Victor-Hugo and the nearby **Haddock Café** at 13 rue de l'Agau (both popular with students).

La Comédie
Hip dance club. *Info: 28 rue Jean-Reboul. Tel. 04/66.76. 13.66.*

Lulu
Gay nightclub. *Info: 10 impasse de la Curaterie. Tel. 04/ 66.36.28.20.*

Orange
Les Chorégies d'Orange
This is an opera and classical music fair held every July at the Théâtre Antique (*see photo below*).

Uzès
Nuits Musicales d'Uzès
Organ concerts are held in the Cathédrale St-Théodorit, especially the last two weeks of July, during this musical festival. The concerts are played on its 2,700-pipe organ which dates back to the 17th century.

4. AVIGNON

HIGHLIGHTS

▲ The place de l'Horloge, the heart of the city

▲ The colossal Papal Palace where two popes ruled and the Cathedral

▲ La Fondation Angladon-Dubrujeaud, with art by Picasso, van Gogh, Degas, Cézanne...

▲ The famous bridge with its four arches

▲ Lovely bistros, cafes, restaurants and hotels

INTRO

In 1309, when Pope Clément V arrived after fleeing the corruption of Rome, the town became the capital of Christendom for 68 years. Although the last pope left in 1377, you're reminded of the **papal legacy** everywhere

COORDINATES

Avignon (population 90,000) is in the south of France. It's 60 miles (100km) inland from the Mediterranean port city of Marseille, 51 miles (82km) northeast of Aix-en-Provence, and 425 miles (685 km) south of Paris.

in modern-day Avignon. Its large student population makes it a vibrant city, unlike most of the small villages of Provence. The students, upscale boutiques and crowded cafés all make Avignon the most cosmopolitan city in Provence.

SIGHTS

A DAY IN AVIGNON

Let's start your day in Avignon near the train station and parking lots at the **Porte de la République**, one of the entries through the massive walls built by the Church. You'll be on **cours Jean-Jaurés**. The tourist office is at 41 cours Jean-Jaurés.

The street turns into rue de la République. It's the main street of Avignon, and is filled with shops.

The **Musée Lapidaire** is at the corner of rue de la République and rue Frédéric Mistral. This museum is located in a Jesuit chapel, and is filled with a collection of sculpture and stonework from the 1st and 2nd centuries. *Info: 27 rue de la*

République. www.musee-lapidaire.org. Tel. 04/90.85.75.38. Open Wed-Mon 10am-1pm and 2pm-6pm. Closed Tue. Admission: €2.

Nearby, at the end of rue Frédéric Mistral, is **La Fondation Angladon-Dubrujeaud**. This museum is filled with the works of Picasso, van Gogh, Degas, Modigliani and Cézanne, to name a few. There's also a collection of furniture and art objects. *Info: 5 rue Laboureur. www.angladon.com. Tel. 04/90.82.29.03. Open Wed-Sun 1pm-6pm. Closed Mon and Tue. (Open Tue in summer.) Admission: €6.*

On rue de la République is the

place de l'Horloge. It's the heart of the city, filled with bistros, cafés, and restaurants. It gets its name from the Gothic clock tower (**Tour du Jacquemart**). Great people-watching! On the square are the City Hall (**Hôtel de Ville**) and the 19th-century **Opéra House**. This square is a great place to take a break.

Just off the place de l'Horloge is the place du Palais (rue Phillipe connects the two places).

At the place du Palais, you'll find the **Palais des Papes** (the colossal Papal Palace). For 68 years, popes ruled from here. *Info: place du Palais. www.palais-des-papes.com. Tel. 04/90.27.50.00. Open daily 9am-5:45pm (Jul until 8pm, Apr-Jun and Aug-Oct until 7pm). Admission: 11€ (including audio guide); under 8 free.*

Also on the square is the **Petit Palais**, the former residence of cardinals and bishops, and home to a museum devoted mostly to Italian paintings and sculptures from Avignon's churches. *Info: place du Palais. www.petit-palais.org. Tel. 04/90.86.44.58. Open Wed-Mon 10am-1pm and 2pm-6pm. Admission: €6.*

The cathedral here is the **Cathédrale Notre-Dame des Doms** with the tombs of two popes who ruled from Avignon. It's topped by the gold statue of the Virgin Mary. *Info: place du Palais. Tel. 04/90.86.81.01. Open daily 9am-noon and 2pm-6pm. Admission: Free.*

After you exit the cathedral (with the cathedral to your back) head right through the gates.

Enter the promenade, and you'll head up into the **Rocher-des-Doms** (Rock of the Domes). You can enjoy the views across the Rhône River from this rocky bluff and garden. Huge pine trees, statues and swans make this a great place to relax. There's a small vineyard down the slope. From here, you can also look down at the four remaining arches of the **Pont**

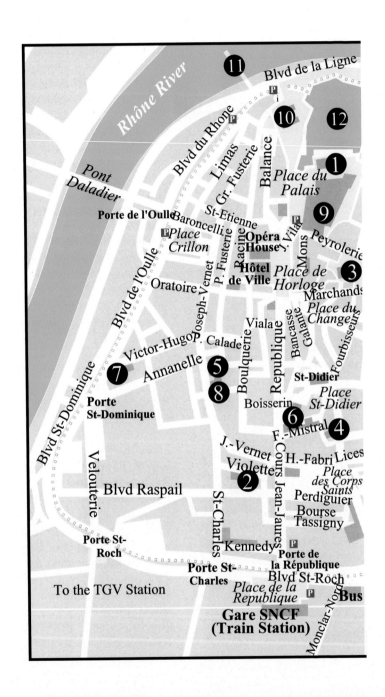

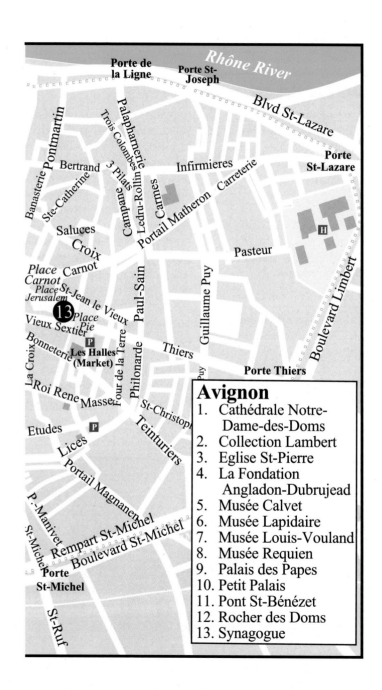

Avignon

1. Cathédrale Notre-Dame-des-Doms
2. Collection Lambert
3. Eglise St-Pierre
4. La Fondation Angladon-Dubrujead
5. Musée Calvet
6. Musée Lapidaire
7. Musée Louis-Vouland
8. Musée Requien
9. Palais des Papes
10. Petit Palais
11. Pont St-Bénézet
12. Rocher des Doms
13. Synagogue

SIGHTS

St-Bénézet (St. Bénézet Bridge) and the ruins in Villeneuve-lès-Avignon across the river.

A WEEKEND IN AVIGNON

Friday Evening
For dinner, you could dine at one of the many cafés, bistros or restaurants on the place de l'Horloge. It's the heart of the city.

After dinner, grab a chair at one of the cafés on the **place de l'Horloge** and watch the world pass you by.

Saturday
Head to the **place du Palais** to begin your day. There are four sights that you can visit here.

Start at the **Papal Palace** (Palais des Papes). In 1309, French Pope Clément V was elected and moved to Avignon from Rome. For 68 years, popes ruled from here. In 1378, there were competing popes (one in Rome and one here). This schism continued until 1417. The popes in Avignon during this schism are referred to as the "antipopes." Benedict XII, the third pope to rule from Avignon, ordered the construction of this colossal palace that dominates Avignon. Today, you can tour the large palace. Be warned, it's mostly empty. The Great Court links the **Palais Vieux** (Old Palace) with the more decorated **Palais Nouveau** (New Palace).

Some highlights are:

- **Chapelle St-Jean**: with its frescoes of the life of John the Baptist
- **Chapelle St-Martial**: with its frescoes of the miracles of St. Martial
- **Banquet Hall** (Grand Tinel): with vaulted roof and 18th-century tapestries
- **Pope's Chamber**: the pontiff slept in this bedroom, whose blue walls are decorated with a vine-leaf motif
- **Council Hall** (Consistoire): with 14th-century frescoes
- **Chambre du Cerf**: featuring murals of a stag hunt and a decorated ceiling
- **Chapelle Clémentine**: where the college of cardinals met
- **Great Audience Hall** (Grande Audience): with frescoes of the prophets

Info: place du Palais. www.palais-des-papes.com. Tel. 04/90.27.50.00. Open daily 9am-5:45pm (Jul until 8pm, Apr-Jun and Aug-Oct until 7pm). Admission: €11 (including audio guide); under 8 free.

Also on the square is the **Petit Palais**. The former residence of cardinals and bishops is now the home of a museum devoted mostly to Italian paintings. Among them are works by Bellini, Botticelli and Carpaccio. *Info: place du Palais. www.petit-palais.org. Tel. 04/90.86.44.58. Open Wed-Mon 10am-1pm and 2pm-6pm. Admission: €6.*

The cathedral here is the **Cathédrale Notre-Dame-des-Doms**. Some of the popes who ruled from the nearby Papal

Palace are buried here in the Gothic tomb. The cathedral dates back to the 12th century. The gold statue of the Virgin that tops the cathedral is from the 19th century. *Info: place du Palais. Tel. 04/90.86.81.01. Open daily 9am-noon and 2pm-6pm. Admission: Free.*

SIGHTS

On the hill next to the cathedral is the **Rocher des Doms** (Rock of the Domes). You can enjoy the views across the Rhône River from this rocky bluff and garden. Huge pine trees, statues and swans make this a great place to relax. *Info: Montée du Moulin (on the hill next to the cathedral). Open daily. Admission: Free.*

From here, you can see the **Pont St-Bénézet** (St. Bénézet Bridge). There's a famous French children's song about this bridge: "*Sur le pont d'Avignon on y danse, on y danse...*" ("On the bridge of Avignon one dances, one dances..."). If that's the case, they better watch where they're stepping, as this arched bridge stretches across only part of the river. Legend has it that a shepherd named Bénézet was told by an angel to begin building the bridge in 1177. Only four arches of the original 22 remain, the rest having been destroyed by floods and war. There's a chapel on the bridge, and a small free museum of the history of the bridge. *Info: rue Ferruce. Open daily 9:30am-5:45pm (Jul-Sep until 8pm). Admission: €4 (audio guide included).*

Head back to the **place de l'Horloge** and take a break from all this sightseeing. Why don't you try a *pastis* (anise-flavored aperitif)? A Provençal word meaning mixture, it's a summer drink. Common brands are Pastis 51, Pernod, Ricard, Granier, Prado and Henri Bardouin.

If you're up for more sightseeing, you have two very different choices:

At **La Fondation Angladon-Dubrujeaud**, designer Jacques Doucet's former home is now a museum filled with works by Picasso, van Gogh, Degas, Modigliani and Cézanne, to name just a few. There's also a collection of furniture and art objects. *Info: 5 rue Laboureur. Tel. 04/90.82.29.03. www.angladon. com. Open Wed-Sun 1pm-6pm. Closed Mon. Open Tue in summer. Admission: €7.*

If you're more interested in antiquities, head to the **Musée Lapidaire**. Among the boutiques on this street you'll find this museum housed in a small Jesuit chapel, filled with sculpture and stonework from the 1st and 2nd centuries. *Info: 27 rue de la République. www.musee-lapidaire.org. Tel. 04/90.85.75.38. Open Wed-Mon 10am-1pm and 2pm-6pm. Closed Tue. Admission: €2.*

If you'd rather part with some cash, shops (from expensive to budget) are found on rue de la République and rue St-Agricole. A favorite shop is **Terre è Provence**, where you'll find beautiful Provençal pottery. *Info: 26 rue de la République. Tel. 04/90.85.56.45. Closed Sun.*

Sunday
Start your day at **Les Halles**. It opens at 6am. This large covered market was built in the 1970s. Stinky fish, stinky cheese and lots of other stuff. *Info: place Pie. Closed Mon.*

Nearby are two places of worship.

At rue Bernheim-Lyon (off of rue du Vieux Sextier) is a **synagogue** dating back to the 1200s. There's a memorial to Jews deported from here to the concentration camp at Auschwitz. *Info: rue Bernheim-Lyon (off of rue du Vieux Sextier). Closed some Sat and Sun. Admission: Free.*

You can admire the Gothic façade of **Eglise St-Pierre**, a 12th-century church. The 16th-century carved doors depict the Annunciation, when the angel Gabrielle informed Mary that she would conceive a son. *Info: place St-Pierre/ rue des Ciseaux d'Or. Open daily. Admission: Free.*

Now how about museums, museums and more museums?

Alternate Plan

One of the largest natural-history libraries in France is located at the **Musée Requien**, but most come to visit its herbarium which contains more than 200,000 specimens gathered by botanists from around the world. There's also an exhibit featuring the botany of Provence. *Info: 67 rue Joseph-Vernet. Tel. 04/90.82.43.51. Closed Sun and Mon. Admission: Free.*

If you're interested in antiquities, visit the **Musée Calvet**. Located in a beautiful 18th-century mansion, this museum (with a lovely garden) maintains a collection of antiquities (some of which are housed at the Musée Lapidaire above), and works by Manet, Brueghel, Corot and David. *Info: 65 rue Joseph-Vernet. Tel. 04/90.86.33.84. www.musee-calvert.org. Open Wed-Mon 10am-1pm and 2pm-6pm. Closed Tue. Admission: €6.*

Another choice for antiquities is the lesser-known **Musée Louis-Vouland**. Located in a 19th-century mansion, this museum is filled with 17th- and 18th-century antiques, tapestries and art objects. *Info: 17 rue Victor-Hugo. Tel. 04/90.86.03.79. Open Tue-Sun noon-6pm (2pm-6pm in winter). Closed Mon. Admission: €4.*

If modern art is more to your liking, head to the **Collection Lambert**. The exterior of this 18th-century mansion doesn't look anything like the contemporary art housed inside. *Info: 5 rue Violette. Tel. 04/90.16.56.20. Open Tue-Sun 11am-6pm. Open daily Jul and Aug 11am-7pm. Admission: €10. www.collection.lambert.com.*

If you want to get away from Avignon but don't want to drive, cross the Rhône River to **Villeneuve-lès-Avignon** (*see photo below*). Villeneuve means "new city" and refers to the area across the **Pont Daladier** from Avignon (bus 11 runs between the two cities). In the 1300s, cardinals built private estates here. The **Fort St-André** dominates the hilltop. The 13th-century **Tour Philippe le Bel** affords great views of Avignon and the Rhône Valley. *Info: rue Montée-de-la-Tour. Tel. 04/32.70.08.57. Open daily Apr-Sep 10am-12:30pm and 2pm-6:30pm. Oct-Nov Tue-Sun 10am-12:30pm and 2pm-5pm. Closed Dec-Feb. Admission: €2.*

At the **Musée de Villeneuve-lès-Avignon**, the former residence of cardinals is now the

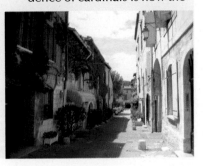

home of a museum loaded with medieval sculpture and paintings. *Info: rue de la République. Tel. 04/90.27.49.66. Open Apr-Sep Tue-Sun 10am-12:30pm and 3pm-7pm. Oct-Mar Tue-Sun 10am-noon and 2pm-5:30pm. Closed Mon and Feb. Admission: €3.*

Built in 1352, **Chartreuse du Val-de-Bénédiction** (*photo at right*) is France's largest monastery. It was founded by Pope Innocent VI, who is buried here. You can visit the church, three cloisters, monastic cells and splendid gardens. *Info: 60 rue de la République. Tel. 04/90.15.24.24. Open daily 9:30am-5:30pm. Admission: €7.*

The **Eglise Notre-Dame** dates back to the 1300s and has lovely statues and a lavish 18th-century altar. *Info: place Meissonier. Tel. 04/90.25.61.55. Open daily 10am-noon and 2pm-5pm. Admission: Free.*

After dinner, end your weekend at the **place de l'Horloge**. Order a flute of champagne (*coupe de champagne*) and toast your great weekend in Avignon.

BEST SLEEPS & EATS

AVIGNON
Hôtel de la Mirande €€€
This 20-room hotel, located in a 700-year-old town house behind the Papal Palace, is luxurious, comfortable and elegant (with a renowned restaurant, too). Rooms are filled with antiques (number 20 is the most sought after). Truly an experience. *Info: 4 place de la Mirande. www.la-mirande.fr. Tel. 04/90.14.20.20. V, MC, DC, AE. Restaurant, bar, TV, AC, telephone, minibar, hairdryer, safe.*

SLEEPS & EATS

Hôtel d'Europe €€-€€€

A hotel since 1799 in a building dating back to the 1580s, this award-winning 44-room hotel is known for its central location, attentive service, and excellent restaurant, "La Vielle Fontaine." Its three suites have private terraces overlooking the Papal Palace. *Info: 14 place Crillon. www.heurope.com. Tel. 04/90.14.76.76. V, MC, DC, AE. Restaurant, bar, TV, AC, telephone, minibar, hairdryer, safe, wireless Internet.*

Cloître St-Louis €€

Located in a historic 16th-century building, this hotel has 80 rooms with modern furnishings, a pool, the restaurant Le St-Louis located under vaulted ceilings, and comfortable lounges. *Info: 20 rue du Portail Boquier. www.cloitre-saint-louis.com. Tel. 04/90.27.55.55. V,*

MC, AE. AC, TV, telephone, minibar, safe, hairdryer, Internet access.

Mercure Pont d'Avignon €€

This hotel, part of a chain (with hotels in Marseille, Aix and Nice), has 87 rooms, all with small bathrooms. Its central location can't be beat as it's near the foot of the Papal Palace. *Info: rue Ferruce. www.mercure.com. Tel. 04/90.80.93.93. V, MC, DC, AE. Bar, TV, AC, telephone, minibar, hairdryer, safe, WiFi.*

Le Médiéval €

Located in an 18th-century town house, this 34-room hotel has an excellent location, only three blocks south of the Papal Palace. Decent-sized rooms with beamed ceilings have tub/shower combinations in the bathrooms. Ask for a room on the courtyard rather than the noisy street. *Info: 15 rue Petite Saunerie. www.hotelmedieval.com. Tel. 04/90.86.11.06. V, MC. TV, telephone, Internet access, hairdryer.*

La Mirande €€€

This renowned restaurant, located in a hotel in a converted 700-year-old town house behind the Papal Palace, offers elegant French dining. *Info: 4 place de la Mirande. www.la-mirande.fr. Tel. 04/90.14.20.20. Reservations required.*

Brunel €€-€€€

This family-owned, elegant bistro is a great spot for lunch or dinner after visiting the Papal Palace. *Info: 46 rue de la Balance. Tel. 04/90.85.24.83. Closed Sun, Mon and part of Aug. Open Mon in July.*

Hiély-Lucullus €€-€€€

Fine French dining, such as grilled lamb and fresh fish, at a lovely

centrally located restaurant. *Info: 5 rue de la République. www.hiely-lucullus.com. Tel. 04/90.86.17.07. Reservations required. Closed Sat (lunch) and part of Aug.*

La Fourchette €€

French cuisine at moderate prices at this cozy restaurant a block from place de l'Horloge. *Info: 7 rue Racine. Tel. 04/90.85.20.93. Closed weekends and part of Aug.*

Le Grand Café €-€€

This popular bistro behind the Papal Palace, is in an entertainment complex with a movie theatre and bar, has interesting industrial décor and good food at reasonable prices. *Info: rue des Escaliers Ste-Anne. Tel. 04/90.86.86.77. Closed Sun, Mon and Jan.*

BEST SHOPPING

Avignon
Les Halles opens at 6am. This large covered market was built in the 1970s. Stinky fish, stinky cheese and lots of other stuff. *Info: place Pie. Closed Mon.*

There is a **flower market** at place des Carmes (Saturday mornings), and a **flea market** at place des Carmes (Sunday mornings).

Terre è Provence
Beautiful Provençal pottery at this interesting shop. *Info: 26 rue de la République. Tel. 04/90.85.56.45. Closed Sun.*

Villeneuve-lès-Avignon
All sorts of antiques and *brocantes* (secondhand goods) available at an outdoor market at place du Marché on Saturday mornings.

BEST NIGHTLIFE & ENTERTAINMENT

Le Grand Café
This popular bar behind the Papal Palace is in an entertainment complex with a movie theatre and bistro. Interesting industrial décor. *Info: rue des Escaliers Ste-Anne. Tel. 04/90.86.86.77. Closed Sun, Mon and Jan. Inexpensive.*

Les Ambassadeurs
Avignon's most popular dance club. *Info: 27 rue Bancasse. Tel.04/90.86.31.55.*

L'Esclav
Gay bar and disco. *Info: 12 rue de Limas, Tel.04/90.85.14.91*

The **Festival d'Avignon**, an annual festival of dance, theater and music is held the last three weeks of July and the first week of August in Avignon. The squares are full of street performers, from good to absolutely awful. Can you say "mimes?" *Info: www.festival-avignon.com.*

5. LUBERON

HIGHLIGHTS
▲ The markets and shops of L'Isle-sur-la-Sorgue

▲ Fontaine-de-Vaucluse, the "Niagara Falls of Provence"

▲ Gordes, Roussillon, Saignon and Lourmain – the latter a true gastronome's delight

INTRO

Just a short distance from Avignon and Aix-en-Provence by car, the towns of the **Luberon** region are my favorites. From canals and antique shops in **L'Isle-sur-la-Sorgue** to fine dining in **Lourmarin** to

COORDINATES

The small towns of the **Luberon region** are just a short distance (20-30 miles [32-48 km]) from Avignon and Aix-en-Provence.

truly unspoiled villages like **Cucuron**, this area offers the perfect vacation. This is the heart of the market area; nearly every town has a great one, and these otherwise quiet towns come to life on market day.

L'Isle-sur-la-Sorgue is called the Venice of Provence; the majestic **Fontaine-de-Vaucluse** is sometimes referred to as the Niagara Falls of Provence. Walk around the picturesque village of **Gordes** and visit other beautiful small towns in the region, with their lavender fields, lovely markets, and wonderful hotels, restaurants and cafés.

SIGHTS

A WEEK IN THE LUBERON

L'Isle-sur-la-Sorgue
Today, we'll visit **L'Isle-sur-la-Sorgue**. It's 16 miles (26 km) east of Avignon/25 miles (40 km) southeast of Orange.

The name means "Island on the Sorgue River," and is often referred to as the "Venice of Provence." I love this valley town. You'll find pedes-

trian bridges with flower boxes crossing graceful canals. Nine moss-covered waterwheels (that once powered the town's paper, silk and wool mills) remain along the canals.

Only Paris is said to have more antique and secondhand shops in France. There are more than 300 shops in this little town. Most are open daily. There's a huge antique fair at Easter. Try **Galerie aux Trouvailles**. This indoor antique center has 20 shops selling everything from furniture to household goods. *Info: 12*

SIGHTS

la Petit Marine. Tel. 04/ 90.21.14.31. Closed Tue and Wed.

You're going to need a break after looking at all those antiques. Head to **Le Caveau de la Tour de l'Isle**, a wine bar and store on the cobblestone, pedestrian-only street leading to the cathedral. You can try wines by the glass with local cheese and sausage. *Info: 12 rue de la République. Tel. 04/ 90.20.70.25. Closed Sun and Mon. Inexpensive.*

In the center of the Old Town, you'll find the **Collégiale Notre-Dame-des-Anges**, a 17th-century church. Its Baroque interior is filled with gilded statues, frescoes and *faux* marble. Parts of the church date back to the 12th century. *Info: Center of Old Town. Open daily. Admission: Free.*

Next to the Collégiale Notre-Dame-des-Anges on the place de la Liberté is the picturesque **Café de France**, another good place for a break.

If you can, stay for dinner in this lovely city. It has many fine places to dine.

Fontaine-de-Vaucluse
While nearby L'Isle-sur-la-Sorgue has been called the "Venice of Provence," **Fontaine-de-Vaucluse** has been called the "Niagara Falls of Provence." It's 5 miles (8 km) east of L'Isle-sur-la-Sorgue/20 miles (32 km) east of Avignon. Parking €3 on both sides of town.

Don't be fooled, though, as at times of the year the *fontaine*, in a cave at the end of a riverside walk, is not much to look at. Europe's most powerful spring gushes 55 million gallons of water each day from the base of 750-feet-high cliffs.

SIGHTS

The source? No one really knows. Millions visit this sight, and the little village of the same name is loaded with souvenir shops and cafés. You'll pass these on your way to the *fontaine* after you pay to park your car. Visit early or late in the day to avoid the crowds. In the evening, the illuminated *château* sparkles above the town.

While here, there are plenty of cafés and restaurants to take a break. There are also several good special-interest museums. The **Speleology Museum** (Écomusée du Gouffre) is a small underground museum devoted to caves, caving, rocks and minerals (45-minute guided tours). *Info: chemin de la Fontaine (the riverside walk to the fountain). Tel. 04/90.20.34.13. Open daily. Closed Dec and Jan. Admission: €5.50.*

The **Musée d'Histoire 1939-1945** is a modern museum devoted to the literature, art and history of World War II, especially the Nazi occupation of France. *Info: chemin de la Fontaine. Tel. 04/90.20.24.00. Closed Tue and Dec 25-May 1. Admission: €5.*

The small **Musée Pétrarque** honors Petrarch, an Italian Renaissance poet who moved here after being rejected by a married woman. *Info: Rive Gauche de la Sorgue (village center). Tel. 04/90.20.37.20. Closed Nov-Mar. Admission: €4.*

Vallis-Clausa is a working paper mill where artisans create paper as done in the 15th-century. *Info: chemin de la Fontaine. Tel. 04/ 90.20.34.14. Open daily. Admission: Free.*

Guided **canoe trips** depart from Fontaine-de-Vaucluse on two-hour, five-mile trips down the Sorgue River. The trip ends in nearby L'Isle-sur-la-Sorgue and a shuttle brings you back. There are several tour companies offering these trips. One is **Kayaks Verts**, *Tel. 04/90.20.35.44, €20.*

Gordes & The Village des Bories
Perched above the Coulon Valley, the small picturesque village of **Gordes** has narrow alleys between stone homes that appear to be stacked on top of each other. It's 10 miles (16 km) southeast of Fontaine-de-Vaucluse/ 22 miles (36 km)

SIGHTS

east of Avignon. Gordes is touristy and trendy, with boutiques and galleries.

In the center of town, you'll find the fortified Renaissance **Château des Gordes**. You can view its interior and a contemporary art collection. *Info: Center of town. Tel. 04/ 90.72.02.75. Closed Tue. Admission: €5.*

Also in the center of town is the **Eglise St-Fermin**. Stop in for a quick view of the church's blue floral interior and *faux* marble pulpit. *Info: Center of town. Open daily. Admission: Free.*

Only two miles away from Gordes is a popular tourist destination, the **Village des Bories**. *Bories* are beehive-shaped stone huts built by peasants (without mortar) who lived in them while tending their flocks. There are said to be 6,000 in Provence. It's believed that Neolithic man

lived in huts like these, and that they were copied over the years. This cluster of *bories* is part of a village showcasing this peasant community, which was inhabited between 1600 and 1800. Note that if you're unable to park in the lot closest to the village, the walk from route D2 is 1.2 miles (2 km). *Info: 2 miles (4 km) southwest of Gordes off route D2 toward Coustellet. Tel. 04/90.72.03.48. Open daily 9am until sunset. Admission: €6.*

Only two miles from Gordes is a must-see sight and worth the drive.

If you're visiting in late June, July or August, the lavender fields surrounding the austere 12th-century abbey **Abbaye Notre-Dame de Sénanque** are in splendid bloom. Even if you don't visit the abbey, don't miss this perfect photo opportunity. You can visit he cloisters, church, refectory

SIGHTS

Colorful Lavender

It's everywhere and it's beautiful. During **lavender season** (late June through August), there's nothing more breathtaking than lavender fields and yellow fields of sunflowers. Lavender is harvested beginning in July and distilled for perfume and soap. Some of the most spectacular lavender fields are found between Buoux and Forcalquier. For those interested in lavender, you can visit the **Musée de la Lavande** on route D2 in Cabrières outside of Gordes.

D177. www.senanque.fr. Tel. 04/90.72.05.72. Open Mon-Sat 10am-noon and 2pm-6pm, Sun 2pm-6pm. Admission: €7.

Roussillon

Today, we'll visit colorful **Roussillon** and experience a taste of old Provence in **Oppède-le-Vieux.** Roussillon is 6 miles (10 km) east of Gordes/28 miles (45 km) east of Avignon.

Legend has it that a local lord had his wife's lover killed and the wife threw herself off a cliff, staining the rocks with her blood. In reality, two centuries of **ochre mining** have left this perched village surrounded by red quarries and cliffs. From deep red to light

and dormitory. The only heated room was the calefactory, or sitting room, which allowed the monks to read and write without freezing. There are permanent exhibits on the history of the Cistercians and the construction of the abbey, and there are still monks who make this their home. *Info: 2 miles (4 km) north of Gordes on route*

SIGHTS

Luberon Hill Towns

D942 · D4 · Fontaine-de-Vaucluse · Gordes · N100 · Isle-sur-la-Sorgue · D22 · D2 · *Village des Bories* · Roussillon · N100 · Cavaillon · Menerbes · Apt · Saignon · Oppède · Bonnieux · Lacoste · Buoux · A7 · LUBERON · Cucuron · D973 · D943 · Lourmarin · Ansouis · D973 · D17 · N7

yellow, the colors of this town alone are worth a visit. Although it can be quite crowded in high tourist season, you can still find peaceful, beautiful squares and take in the surrounding countryside.

Just three miles (five km) southeast of Roussillon on route D108 is the **Pont Julien**. This three-arched bridge was built by the Romans over 2000 years ago without the use of mortar. It crosses the Calavon River.

While Roussillon is usually crowded with tourists, the nearby town of **Oppède-le-Vieux** will give you a taste of Old Provence. It's 9 miles (14

km) south of Gordes/16 miles (26 km) southeast of Avignon.

This hilltop village (don't confuse it with the lower modern town of Oppède), surrounded by thick forests, was deserted in 1900. The ruins of a medieval *château* loom above. In fact, much of the town itself is still in ruins, although some artists and writers have moved in and beautifully restored homes. You must park at the base of the hill (*€2*) and walk

SIGHTS

through a tiered garden filled with local plants labeled with their Latin, French and English names. Cross through the old city gate and walk up the steep alleys to visit the 13th-century church **Notre-Dame d'Alydon**, with its gargoyles and hexagon-shaped bell tower. Truly a taste of old Provence.

Outside of the old city gate are two places to stop for a drink or a bite. **Le Petit Café** and **L'Echauguette** both have decent fare at reasonable prices.

**Ménerbes & The Land of
*A Year in Provence***
Peter Mayle wrote *A Year in Provence* about **Ménerbes** and the towns surrounding it. Ménerbes is 3 miles (5 km) east of Oppède-le-Vieux/19 miles (31 km) southeast of Avignon.

This town with its impressive

fortifications and crowned by the turreted *château* was once a Protestant stronghold during the 16th-century War of the Religions. You'll find Renaissance homes and terrific views of the countryside. Visit the attractive **Place de l'Horloge** (Clock Square), in the shadow of City Hall.

Although Picasso once owned a home in Ménerbes, it's another home that gets all the attention. Peter Mayle wrote the enormously successful *A Year in Provence* about his home and the towns surrounding it. Tour buses still pass by and gawk. He no longer lives here and it's hard to feel sorry for the current owners as they must have known what they were getting themselves into! *Info: 1 mile (2 km) from Ménerbes on route D3 to Bonnieux (second house from the right after the soccer field). No admission.*

Between Oppède-le-Vieux and Ménerbes is the **Musée du Tire-Bouchon** (Corkscrew Museum). Housed in a mansion, this museum doesn't just feature thousands of corkscrews. It also has wine tastings. *Info: On route D109 between Oppède-le-Vieux* and *Ménerbes. Tel. 04/ 90.72.41.58. Closed Sun in wnter. Admission: €4.*

Just four miles (six km) east of Ménerbes is **Lacoste**. This town with its fortified medieval gateways is dominated by the *château* that was once owned by the Marquis de Sade who hosted his infamous orgies here. The castle is currently being restored by designer Pierre Cardin. The town comes to life in July and August when the **Festival Lacoste**, with musical and theatrical events, takes place.

When visiting this area, don't miss the hilltop village of **Bonnieux**. It's 3 miles (5km) east of Lacoste/7 miles (11 km) southeast of Rousillon/28 miles (46 km) northwest of Aix-en-Provence (*photo below*).

Layers of homes topped with a 12th-century church (the simply named **Vieille Eglise** or "Old Church") make Bonnieux one of the most impressive hilltop villages. Its steep streets are bordered by restored homes. Climb the 86 steps from the place de la Liberté and rue de la Mairie up to the church to take in the great view of the surrounding countryside.

While here, I recommend **Le Fournil** where you can dine outdoors.

There's nothing like French bread. The **Musée de la**

SIGHTS

Boulangerie, in a 17th-century house, features a century-old bread oven and bread shop. Exhibits show all phases of breadmaking. *Info: 12 rue de la République. Tel. 04/90.75.88.34. Open 10am-noon and 2pm-6pm.Closed Tue and Nov-Mar. Admission: €4.*

Near Bonnieux is an excellent setting for dinner. Provençal specialties are served at **Auberge de l'Aiguebrun** or, if you want to visit one of Peter Mayle's favorites in *A Year in Provence*, head to the small town of **Buoux**, five miles (nine km) south of Apt. This peaceful rural town is surrounded by lavender fields and crowned by the ruins of the Buoux Fort. It's a destination for the popular **Auberge de la Loube** restaurant, where *agneau rôti* (roast lamb) is the specialty.

Apt & Saignon

Today we'll visit the market town of **Apt** and the unspoiled village of **Saignon**. Apt is 32 miles (52 km) northwest of Aix-en-Provence/32 miles (52 km) west of Avignon.

Apt's claim to fame, despite its unattractive industrial outskirts, is that it's the world capital of candied fruit (*fruits-confits*). You'll find shops selling it everywhere. There's a huge market on Saturday mornings at **place de la Bouquerie**. The **Old Town** (Vieille Ville) with its narrow streets is worth a visit. The **Cathédrale St-Anne** (closed Sunday afternoons) in the Old Town has a large collection of relics (guided tours only), and the cathedral's crypt is said to hold the remains of St. Anne, the mother of the Virgin Mary.

Near the ancient cathedral are three museums: **Maison du Parc** (a geology museum), **Musée de la Paléontologie** (a dinosaur museum), and **Musée**

de l'Aventure Industrielle (a museum dedicated to the local candied-fruit, ochre-extraction and earthenware industries). The town also has an **Archeology Museum** (Musée Archéologique) at place Carnot with Roman objects from the surrounding area. *Info: Closed Tue. Admission: €3.*

Nearby is the truly unspoiled hill town of **Saignon**. It's two miles (three km) southeast of Apt. Out of the way, but certainly worth the trip! This lovely, quiet, and unspoiled town high on a hill has picturesque shady squares, time-worn fountains and ruins of ancient baths. The wood-carved doors of the Roman church **Eglise Notre-Dame de Pitié** depict Christ and Mary. The cemetery behind the church provides its permanent "residents" with a panoramic view of the countryside.

Lourmarin

Hungry? Head to **Lourmarin**, the gastronomic capital of Provence. It's six miles (ten km) south of Bonnieux.

Lourmarin's winding narrow streets are lined with stone houses painted in shades of ochre and beige. It has a Renaissance chapel and both Catholic and Protestant churches. The village lies at the foot of the Luberon Mountain range which is covered with pine and oak trees. Surrounding the village are olive groves and vineyards. Although French vacationers discovered this little village years ago, it's now popular with foreign tourists. Its renovated *château* is the site of frequent concerts and exhibits. Visitors have quite a few cafés and restaurants to choose from, and it's become the gastronomic capital of the area. It's a lovely town with much to offer, and a great base for touring some of the prettiest towns of Provence.

When in town, head to **La Cave à Lourmarin**. The interesting wines of the Côtes du Luberon, along with regional products, are available at incredibly discounted prices at this shop in the center of town. Friendly

SIGHTS

and helpful staff and generous wine tastings. *Info: Montée du Galinier. Tel. 04/90.68.02.18. Open daily.*

There are two towns nearby that are worth the short drives. **Cucuron** is only four miles (seven km) east of Lourmarin. Tourism has yet to invade this scenic small town. Parts of the ancient walls survive. A fortified gate and bell tower on place de l'Horloge is the entry for the ruins above the town. Take a break with locals at cafés along the large stone pool (**Bassin de l'Etang**) dating back to the 15th century.

Most Beautiful Villages

There are 141 villages throughout France designated as **Plus Beaux Villages** (Most Beautiful Villages). In order to receive this designation, the village must have a population under 2,000 and have at least two sites or buildings designated as "protected" by the government.

The villages featured in this book are: Moustiers-Ste-Marie, Gourdon, Les Baux-de-Provence, Ansouis, Gordes, Lourmarin, Ménerbes, Roussillon, Séguret, and Gassin.

There's a large market here on Tuesday mornings. The church **Eglise Notre-Dame-de-Beaulieu** has Gothic chapels and a Baroque altarpiece. Near the church is an ancient olive press, **Moulin à Huile Dauphin**, with a shop selling local specialties.

Ansouis is only eight miles (ten km) southeast of Lourmarin; the town lies at the foot of its **medieval castle** (*photo below*). The village houses are spread over the southern slope to shelter them from the Mistral (the brutal winds that touch this area at certain times of the year). There's a 16th-century tower crowned with a wrought-iron bell tower, and the castle with its fortified walls and watchtower has been restored (guided visits only in the afternoons). Wooded groves, gardens and terraces surround the castle. You can pop into the church **Eglise St-Martin**. Originally a 12th-century fortress and former law court,

this small church contains 17th- and 18th-century statues and altar pieces. At the entry to the castle, you can stop into the information center and purchase an inexpensive bottle of local wine.

Gardeners must visit **La Ferme de Gerbaud**, a 62-acre farm on the slopes of the Luberon mountain range offering 90-minute guided tours in English and French. You'll see aromatic herbs and regional plants. The shop sells fragrances, dyes, olive oils and herbs. *Info: 2 miles (3 km) outside of Lourmarin (chemin d'Aguye to chemin de Gerbaud). Tel. 04/ 90.68.11.83. Tours Apr-Oct Tue, Thu and Sat at 5pm, Nov-Mar Sun at 3pm. Admission: €5.*

BEST SLEEPS & EATS

BONNIEUX
Auberge de l'Aiguebrun €€
Provençal specialties at this farmhouse located in a small valley near Bonnieux. Great food in an excellent setting. *Info: 4 miles*

(6 km) southeast of Bonnieux (near the intersection of routes D36 and D943). www.auberge delaiguebrun.fr. Tel. 04/ 90.04.47.00 for the inn /04/ 90.71.72.27 for the restaurant. Closed Tue and Wed (lunch).

Le Fournil €€
Dine outdoors by the 12th-century fountain or inside in a grotto at this former bakery. Provençal cuisine and a great wine list. *Info: 5 place Carnot. Tel. 90.75.83.62. Closed Mon, Tue (lunch), Sat (lunch), Dec, Jan to mid-Feb and mid-Nov to mid-Dec.*

BUOUX
Auberge de la Loube €€€
This restaurant gained renown in Peter Mayle's *A Year in Provence*. The Provençal fare won't disappoint, especially the lamb. Dining is on the comfortable covered patio. Try the *agneau rôti* (roast

SLEEPS & EATS

lamb). *Info: Quartier la Loube. Tel. 04/90.74.19.58. Closed Mon, Thu and Jan. No credit cards.*

GORDES
La Bastide €€-€€€
This 45-unit inn – suites are the most expensive–is located in one

of the stone homes that appear to be stacked on top of each other here. Tastefully decorated rooms, attentive staff, and a luxurious pool all make this a perfect base to explore the area. *Info: Le Village. www.bastide-de-gordes.com. Tel. 04/90.72.12.12. V, MC, DC, AE. Restaurant, bar, gym, AC, TV, telephone, minibar, in-room safe, hairdryer, Internet access.*

Comptoir du Victuailler €€
This small, 1930s-style bistro serves wonderful roast meats (especially lamb). Garlic mayonnaise (*aïoli*), a Provençal specialty, is featured in many dishes. *Info: place du Château (across from the château). Tel. 04/90.72.01.31. Closed Tue (dinner) and Wed in winter. Closed mid-Nov to mid-Dec.*

La Bastide €€€
This restaurant is located in an inn of the same name. Provençal and Mediterranean dishes are served on the lovely terrace. Attentive staff. *Info: Le Village. Tel. 04/90.72.12.12. www.bastide-de-gordes.com. Fixed-priced menu. Open daily for lunch and dinner.*

L'ISLE-SUR-LA-SORGUE
Hostellerie la Grangette €€-€€€
Lots of charm at this peaceful, vine-covered inn surrounded by oak trees just three miles north of town in Velleron. Fantastic pool. Rooms have tiled floors and are tastefully decorated with antiques from the markets in L'Isle-sur-la-Sorgue. Excellent lunch

or dinner on the terrace (reservations required). *Info: Chemin Cambuisson in Velleron. www.lagrangette-provence.com. Tel. 04/90.20.00.77. V, MC. Restaurant, outdoor pool, telephone, wireless Internet access. Closed mid-Nov to mid-Feb.*

La Bastide Rose €€-€€€

This pink villa is located next to a canal. There's a wonderful pool, river views, and an old mill turned into the Pierre Salinger Museum (the owner used to be married to JFK's press secretary). There are five rooms (all have large bathrooms), two suites and a cottage for rent. *Info: 99 Chemin des Croupières in Le Thor (just outside of town). www.bastiderose.com. Tel. 04/90.02.14.33. V, MC, AE. Restaurant, AC, TV, telephone, minibar, in-room safe, hairdryer, Internet access.*

Lou Nego Chin €-€€

I've enjoyed Provençal fare in both the tiny restaurant and outdoors next to the canal. You can sip local wines while the ducks float by and colored lights twinkle above you. Just the type of dining experience you came to Provence for. *Info: 12 quai Jean Jaurès. Tel. 04/90.20.88.03. Closed Wed. Closed Tue in Jul and Aug.*

Le Jardin du Quai €€€

This popular restaurant serves innovative dishes. In good weather, you can dine in its large and lovely garden under chestnut trees. Friendly service. *Info: 91 avenue Julien Guigue (opposite the station). Tel. 04/90.20.14.98.*

SLEEPS & EATS

La Prévôte €€€

Splurge on award-winning cuisine in a lovely setting on a narrow street near the cathedral. Try the duck. *Info: 4 bis rue Jean-Jacques-Rousseau. www.la-prevote.fr/. Tel. 04/90.38.57.29. Closed Tue and Wed and mid-Feb to mid-Mar.*

LOURMARIN

Les Olivettes €€

Les Olivettes offers luxury accomodations of private apartments in a newly renovated farmhouse in the Luberon. It has spectacular views, a large heated swimming-pool, private gardens and, most of all, a relaxing and peaceful atmosphere. English-speaking Joe and Elisabeth Deliso are the perfect hosts. It's an ideal base for visiting the villages of the Luberon. *Info: Ave. Henri Bosco (off of route 27). www.olivettes.com. Tel. 04/90.68.03.52. Weekly rentals. V, MC. Outdoor pool. Kitchens, TV, telephone, minibar, Internet access. Closed Dec-Feb.*

Restaurant Michel Ange €€

In a town known for its restaurants, this is only one choice of many. Outdoor dining on a quiet covered patio. Try the delicious *fleurs des courgettes farcies* (zucchini flowers stuffed with cheese). *Info: place de la Fontaine. Tel. 04/90.68.02.03.*

Auberge La Fenière €€€

Chef Reine Sammut is called the "Queen of Provençal cooking." Experience her innovative dishes at this restaurant on the outskirts of town. *Info: Route de Cadenet. Tel. 04/90.68.11.79. Open daily in high season.*

Le Bistro de Roussillon €€

Indoor and outdoor dining at this friendly bistro serving hearty Provençal fare. *Info: place de la Marine. Tel. 04/90.05.74.45. Closed Jan and mid-Nov to mid-Dec.*

SAIGNON

Auberge du Presbytère €-€€

A lovely hotel in the center of an unspoiled town. Enjoy outdoor dining among the vine-covered stone buildings near the rustic fountain. The 12 rooms–several with terraces – have been recently renovated. Hospitable staff. A range of sizes and prices for rooms. Regional specialties are served at the restaurant. Enjoy outdoor dining among the vine-covered stone buildings near the rustic fountain.*Info: place de la Fontaine. www.auberge-presbytere.com. Tel. 04/90.74.11.50. V, MC, AE. Restaurant, bar. Closed mid-Jan to mid-Feb. Restaurant closed Wed.*

BEST SHOPPING

L'Isle-sur-la-Sorgue
Galerie aux Trouvailles
This indoor antique center has 20 shops selling everything from furniture to household goods. *Info: 12 la Petit Marine. Tel. 04/90.21.14.31. Closed Tue and Wed.*

This otherwise quiet town is filled with crowds on **Sunday**. Stands loaded with local produce, crafts and antiques fill the streets along with street performers. There's a more sedate market on Thursdays. *Info: From the place Gambetta (the main entrance to the town) up avenue des 4 Otages.*

Apt
There's a huge market on **Saturday mornings** at place de la Bouquerie. Especially good for purchasing candied fruit (*fruits-confits*), for which the town is known.

Cucuron
There's a large market here on **Tuesday mornings**.

Lourmarin
In addition to the **Friday-morning market** in Lourmarin,

La Cave à Lourmarin sells interesting wines of the Côtes du Luberon, along with regional products, at incredibly discounted prices at this shop in the center of town. Friendly and helpful staff and generous wine tastings. *Info: Montée du Galinier (in town). Tel. 04/ 90.68.02.18. Open daily.*

6. AIX-EN-PROVENCE

HIGHLIGHTS

▲ A walk down the cours Mirabeau, Aix's lovely main street

▲ Quartier Mazarin, filled with elegant townhouses

▲ The huge market at place Verdun

▲ Musée Granet/Musée des Beaux-Arts, home to eight Cézanne paintings

INTRO

Aix (pronounced "X") is a graceful and sophisticated city. Between the 12th and 15th centuries it was the capital of Provence. The Romans called it "Aquae Sextius" (Waters of Sextius) after the thermal springs that flow here and

COORDINATES

Aix-en-Provence (population 130,000) is in the south of France. It's 19 miles (31km) northeast of the Mediterranean port city of Marseille, 51 miles (82km) southeast of Avignon, and 474 miles (760km) south of Paris.

the Roman general (Caius Sextius Calvinus) who founded the city.

Shaded squares with bubbling fountains in the Old Quarter, 17th-century town houses and the **cours Mirabeau** (the grand main avenue) make Aix a must for all visitors to Provence. It's a cultural center enhanced by thousands of students who attend one of France's oldest universities. It's the hometown of the artist **Paul Cézanne**, who created many of his best-known works here.

SIGHTS

A DAY IN AIX

Start at the tourist office and parking areas at place Général-de-Gaulle at the Rotonde traffic circle.

The black-and-white **marble fountain** at place Général-de-Gaulle (in the middle of the traffic circle) dates back to the 19th century, and features the figures of Fine Art, Agriculture and Justice at the top.

From here, you'll walk down the **cours Mirabeau**. This broad street lined with plane trees and stone buildings was built in the 17th century. You'll pass elegant buildings, four

fountains, and many cafés and shops. This is the heart of Aix. One of the grand mansions on this street, the impressive **Hôtel Maurel de Pontèves** (now the Tribunal of Commerce) with its sculpted figures is at number 38 (on the corner).

In the middle of the cours Mirabeau is the **Fontaine**

Moussue (it means "Mossy Fountain" – you'll understand why when you see it).

If you exit the cours Mirabeau onto rue du 4 Septembre, you'll enter the **Quartier Mazarin**.

It was here that Aix nobility built elegant town houses in the 17th and 18th centuries. After a short walk, you'll be at **place des Quatre Dauphins** dominated by its Baroque fountain.

Two sights of interest in the Quartier Mazarin: The **Musée Granet/Musée des Beaux-Arts** is located in a former priory and is home to a collection of European art from the 16th to 19th centuries. You'll find eight Cézanne paintings here, along with a collection of his drawings and watercolors. *Info: place St-Jean-de-Malte on rue Cardinale. Tel. 04/ 42.52.88.32. Open Jun-Sep 11am-7pm, Oct-Mar noon-6pm. Closed Mon. Admission: €4.*

Next to the museum is one of Aix's many churches. Drop in for a quick view of **Eglise St-Jean-de-Malte.** This Gothic church and chapel of the

Knights of Malta (a charitable organization) is home to the tombs of the counts of Provence. *Info: rue Cardinale and rue d'Italie. Open daily. Admission: Free.*

Head from here to **Old Town**, with its maze of streets and shops, on the other side of the cours Mirabeau.

If you're here on Tuesday, Thursday or Saturday mornings, you'll run into a huge **market** at place Verdun where you can buy anything from antiques to clothes.

Here in the square is the **Palais de Justice**, an **obelisk**, and the Baroque church **Eglise de la Madeleine**.

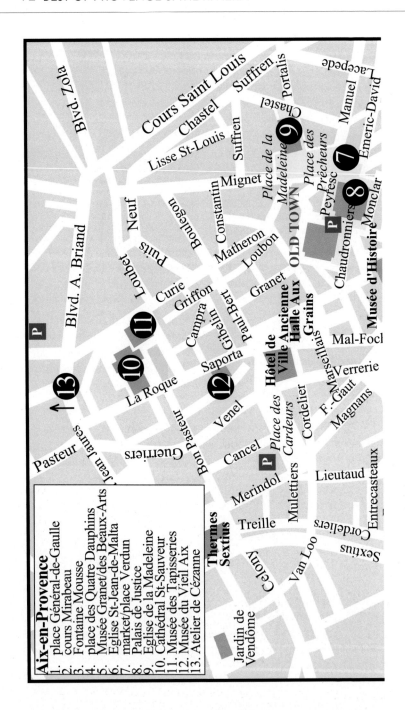

Aix-en-Provence
1. place Général-de-Gaulle
2. cours Mirabeau
3. Fontaine Mousse
4. place des Quatre Dauphins
5. Musée Granet/des Beaux-Arts
6. Eglise St-Jean-de-Malta
7. market/place Verdun
8. Palais de Justice
9. Eglise de la Madeleine
10. Cathédral St-Sauveur
11. Musée des Tapisseries
12. Musée du Vieil Aix
13. Atelier de Cézanne

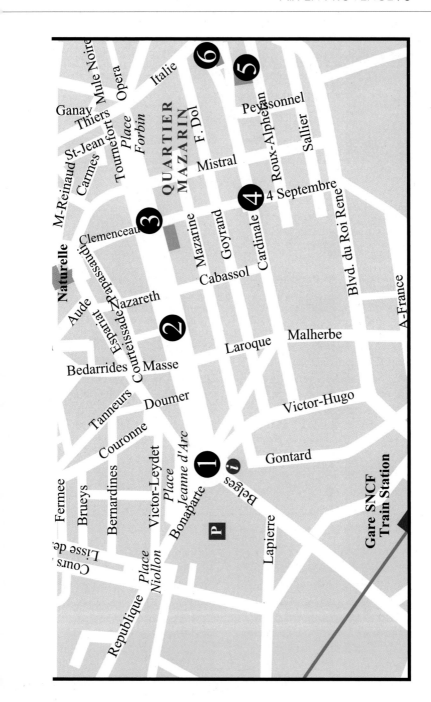

SIGHTS

From place Verdun, find the **Passage Agard** (it has the words "Agard" written above it). It's a covered passageway lined with shops. Go through the passage and when you exit, you'll be back on the cours Mirabeau.

To your right as you exit the passage (at 53 cours Mirabeau) you can stop for coffee or a snack at one of the sidewalk tables at **Brasserie Les Deux Garçons**. This 19th-century brasserie has been a meeting place for intellectuals and writers for years. Today, you'll also find quite a few tourists.

A WEEKEND IN AIX

Friday Evening

It's your first evening in Aix, so head out for a leisurely evening dinner. After dinner, head to the **cours Mirabeau**. There are many cafés along this broad street where you can have a nightcap.

After dinner, head to the **cours Mirabeau**. There are many cafés along this broad street where you can have nightcap.

Saturday

You'll find clothes, antiques and produce at the colorful

Aix Market held in place de Verdun and place des Prêcheurs. It's open Saturday, Tuesday and Thursday mornings.

At place de Verdun is the **Palais de Justice**. On the adjoining place des Prêcheurs is the **Eglise de la Madeleine**. Formerly a Dominican convent, this Baroque church is the site of frequent classical concerts. *Info: place des Prêcheurs (off of place de la Madeleine). Open daily. Admission: Free.*

You're in the **Old Town**. Not too far from here is another church of note.

On the rue Gaston-de-Saporta (the heart of Old Town), the cathedral **Cathédral St-Sauveur** has a 5th-century baptistery, 12th-century cloisters and a 15th-century triptych (three-paneled painting), *The Burning Bush*. The famous triptych is only open for special occasions, however, to protect it from further deterioration. Near the triptych is another three-paneled painting of Christ's passion. The fantastic gilt organ is Baroque, and the tapestries surrounding the

choir date from the 18th century. *Info: rue Gaston-de-Saporta at place des Martyrs de la Résistance. Admission: Free.*

Next to the cathedral is the **Musée des Tapisseries**. This 17th-century archbishop's palace is home to a museum of 17th- and 18th-century tapestries and furnishings. *Info: 28 place des Martyrs de la Résistance. Tel. 04/42.23.09.91. Open Wed-Mon 10am-noon and 2pm-6pm. Closed Tue. Admission: €3.*

Also in Old Town is the **Musée du Vieil Aix** (Museum of Old Aix). This beautiful 17th-century mansion is more

SIGHTS

interesting than the museum of furniture and objects it houses. *Info: 17 rue Gaston-de-Saporta. Tel. 04/42.21.43.55. Open Tue-Sun 10am-1pm and 2pm-6pm (Oct-Mar until 5pm). Closed Mon. Admission: €4.*

Head to the **cours Mirabeau**. This broad street lined with plane trees and stone buildings was built in the 17th century. You'll pass elegant buildings, four fountains, and many cafés and shops.

At 53 cours Mirabeau you can stop for coffee or a snack at one of the sidewalk tables at **Brasserie Les Deux Garçons**. This 19th-century eatery has long been a popular meeting place.

After your break, head into the **Quartier Mazarin**. It was here where Aix nobility built elegant town houses in the 17th and 18th centuries.

There are two sights here (next to each other) that you can easily visit.

The **Musée Granet/Musée des Beaux-Arts** is located in a former priory and is home to a collection of European art from the 16th to 19th centuries. You'll find eight Cézanne paintings here, along with a collection of his drawings and watercolors. *Info: place St-Jean-de-Malte on rue Cardinale. Tel. 04/42.52.88.32. Open Jun-Sep 11am-7pm, Oct-Mar noon-6pm. Closed Mon. Admission: €4.*

Next door is the **Eglise St-Jean-de-Malte**. This Gothic church and chapel of the Knights of Malta (a charitable organization) is home to the tombs of the counts of Provence. *Info: rue Cardinale and rue d'Italie. Open daily. Admission: Free.*

Jazz lovers flock to Aix for a world-renowned **Jazz Festival** held annually at the end of July. Even if you're not here during the annual jazz festival, you can head for **Scat Club** at

11 rue de la Verrerie for some late-night jazz. *Info: Tel.04/42.23.00.23.*

Sunday

The artist Paul Cézanne is from Aix, and created many of his best-known works here. You can start you day by visiting his studio, the **Atelier de Cézanne**. It's located just north of the Old Town. Cézanne painted some of his best-known works here. Americans paid to have his studio restored, and you'll find it much like he left it in 1906.

Info: 9 avenue Paul-Cézanne. www.atelier-cezanne.com. Tel. 04/42.21.06.53. Open daily Apr-Jun and Sep 10am-noon and 2pm-6pm, Jul and Aug 10am-6pm, Oct-Mar 10am-noon and 2pm-5pm. Tours in English at 4pm (Oct-Mar) and 5pm (Apr-Sep. Closed Sun Dec-Feb. Admission: €6.

On Sunday, you could also head outside of Aix to one of two nearby towns.

Meyrargues is 11 miles (19 km) northeast of Aix-en-Provence. This village was a Celtic outpost in 600 B.C. It's dominated by a fortress that was transformed into a *château* in the 17th century and then into an 11-room luxury hotel in the 1950s. Most come to stay at the castle/hotel. They won't mind if you look around the castle and its grounds. The village is charming (despite some bad 1960s apartment buildings in one section). You'll find sweeping views from the castle, along with the remains of a Roman aqueduct in the valley below. *Info: Château de Meyragues, www.chateau-de-meyrargues.com.*

Salon-de-Provence is 23 miles (37 km) northwest of Aix-en-Provence/29 miles (47 km) southeast of Avignon/33 miles (53 km) northwest of Marseille.

This is the hometown of Nostradamus, who is credited with predicting much of the modern era. There's a museum dedicated to him at the **Maison de Nostradamus** at 11 rue Nostradamus (*Tel 04/90.56.64.31, open daily, English audioguide available, admission: €5*). It's a busy, commercial town, center of the region's olive oil industry, and home to the French Air Force.

Children might enjoy the **Grevin Wax Museum** at place du Puits de Jacob, although much of it's dedicated to the history of Provence. *Info: Tel. 04/90.56.36.60, open daily, English audioguide available, admission: €5.* There's a castle looming over the city, **Château de l'Empéri**, that houses a military museum, **Musée d'Art et d'Histoire Militaire**. *Info: Tel. 04/90.44.72.80. Closed Tue. Admission: €5.*

BEST SLEEPS & EATS

Villa Gallici €€€

A stylish and sumptuous hotel located in a garden just a short walk from the cours Mirabeau. Many of the 22 rooms have their

own patios. Pleasant outdoor pool. *Info: avenue de la Violette. Tel. 04/42.23.29.23. www.villagallici.com. V, MC, DC, AE. Restaurant, bar, AC, TV, telephone, minibar, safe.*

Grand Hôtel Nègre Coste €-€€

Smack dab in the middle of the cours Mirabeau, this traditional hotel is a little faded, but certainly worth considering. Rooms are medium-sized and have soundproof windows. Some have great views of the cours Mirabeau, Aix's main street. *Info: 33 cours Mirabeau. www.hotelnegrecoste.com. Tel. 04/42.27.74.22. V, MC, AE. AC, TV, minibar, hairdyer, safe.*

Hôtel Cardinal €

Located in the Quartier Mazarin filled with elegant town houses, this 29-room hotel (and nearby annex) is a good value with basic, comfortable rooms, a helpful staff and a great location. *Info: 24 rue Cardinale. www.hotel-cardinal-aix.com. Tel. 04/42.38.32.30. V, MC. TV, hairdyer.*

Hôtel des Quatre Dauphins €
Also located in the quiet Quartier Mazarin, this small, 13-room hotel is another good value with basic, comfortable accommodations and a great location. *Info: 54 rue Roux-Alphéran. www.lesquatredauphins.fr. Tel. 04/42.38.16.39. V, MC. TV.*

Le Passage €€€
This restaurant, in a former candy factory, gets its name from the

mezzanine dining room that serves as a passage between two streets. You'll be served contemporary Provençal dishes. There's also a cookbook shop, food store, wine shop, tearoom and cooking school. *Info: 6 bis rue Mazarine/10 rue Villars. www.le-passage.fr. Tel. 04/42.37.09.00. Open daily (no lunch). Sunday brunch.*

Antoine Côte Cour €€-€€€
Dine on Provençal and Italian dishes in an 18th-century town house. Try the *osso buco* (braised veal shank). *Info: 19 cours Mirabeau. Tel. 04/42.93.12.51. Closed Sun and Mon (lunch).*

Chez Maxime €€
On the pleasant place Ramus, this restaurant serves Provençal cuisine with an emphasis on grilled meats and fish. Friendly service. *Info: 12 place Ramus. Tel. 04/42.26.28.51. Closed Sun and Mon.*

Mitch €€
Innovative cuisine served in a stone-walled restaurant and on the

patio. *Info: 26 rue des Tanneurs (at avenue Aumône Vieille). Tel. 04/42.26.63.08. Closed Sun.*

Brasserie Les Deux Garçons €€
This 19th-century *brasserie* has waiters in aprons, a beautiful interior and great people-watching from its sidewalk tables along the cours Mirabeau. Standard *brasserie* fare. *Info: 53 cours Mirabeau. Tel. 04/42.26.00.51. Open daily.*

BEST SHOPPING

Le Passage is a food store, wine shop, restaurant, cookbook shop, wine bar, tearoom and cooking school. *Info: 6 bis rue Mazarine/10 rue Villars. Tel. 04/42.37.09.00. Open daily.*

You'll find clothes, antiques and produce at the colorful **Aix Market**, held in place de Verdun and place des

Prêcheurs. *Info: Tue, Thu, and Sat mornings.*

BEST NIGHTLIFE & ENTERTAINMENT

Scat Club
Late-night jazz, blues, rock and world-music performances. *Info: 11 rue de la Verrerie. Tel.04/42.23.00.23.*

Casino Municipal
If you're tired of museums and cafés, try your luck at the casino.*Info: 2 bis avenue Bonaparte.*

The Bistrot Aixois
The most popular dance club in Aix, filled with university students. *Info: 37 cours Sextius. Tel. 04/42.27.50.10.*

Mediterranean Boy
Gay nightclub. *Info: 6 rue de la Paix. Tel.04/42.27.21.47 (bar)*

BEST SPORTS & RECREATION

Le Golf de la Sainte Victoire
Designed by Robert Trent Jones, this prestigious golf club is located in nearby Fuveau, only 7 miles (12km) from Aix. *Info: Chemin Maurel in Fuveau (route D6). Tel. 04/42.29.83.43.*

7. ARLES

HIGHLIGHTS
▲ Espace Van Gogh, Roman ruins

▲ Old Town in St. Rémy

▲ Les Baux de Provence, a delightful medieval hilltop village with great views

▲ Flamingos and birds in the Parc Regional de Camargue

INTRO

On the banks of the Rhône River, **Arles** is one of the three "A's" that make up the most visited cities in Provence (along with Aix-en-Provence and Avignon). Arles has everything you could want in a Provence city: festivals, an Old Town, Roman ruins, cafés (especially on **place du Forum**) and intimate restaurants.

COORDINATES

Arles (population 50,000) is in the south of France. It's 57 miles (92km) inland from the Mediterranean port city of Marseille, 22 miles (36km) south of Avignon, and 450 miles (752km) south of Paris.

Since Arles is situated at the head of the Rhône delta, it's on the route that linked Italy and Spain. When the Romans came into possession of Spain, Arles became an important and strategic town for them. Bullfights, still held in the arena, are a reminder of Arles's Spanish connection. The folk culture and traditions of Arles are alive and well, and you'll see locals dressed in traditional Arlesian costumes on many occasions. **Van Gogh** came here in 1888 and created some of his best-known paintings. Look around and you'll notice that many of the scenes featured in those paintings remain today.

A WEEK IN & AROUND ARLES

Let's first follow in the footsteps of Van Gogh. On our second day, we'll hit the major sights of Arles.

Begin your day with a trip to the **Espace van Gogh**. This is where Vincent van Gogh was sent after he is said to have cut off part of his left ear. The courtyard, which is open to the public, has been landscaped to match van Gogh's famous painting *Le Jardin de l'Hôtel-Dieu*. The building was formerly a hospital. Today it's a cultural center with a wing dedicated to van Gogh that houses an art exhibit. *Info: place Dr. Félix Ray. Open daily. Admission: Free.*

SIGHTS

Now head to place du Forum. You can take a break at one of the many cafés, including **Café de la Nuit**. It's the one that looks like a vibrant van Gogh painting. Great people-watching here!

After taking a break, walk to the area around the arena where you'll find the **Fondation van Gogh**. The name of this small gallery is slightly deceiving. There are no van Gogh paintings here (or for that matter in all of Arles). The gallery exhibits works of major contemporary artists paying homage to van Gogh in re-creations of his works. When van Gogh and fellow painter Paul Gauguin worked together here in 1888, they were treated rather badly. This gallery seems to be an attempt to correct that wrong. *Info: 24 bis Rond Point des Arènes (facing the arena). www.fondationvangogh.org. Tel. 04/90.49.94.04. Open daily 10am-6pm. Admission: €7.*

If you haven't had enough art, you can visit the **Musée Réattu**. This art museum is named after Provençal artist Jacques Réattu. In addition to his works and some 16th-century tapestries, you'll find drawings, etchings and paintings by such notables as Picasso and Gauguin. *Info: rue du Grand Prieuré. Tel. 04/90.49.37.58. Open 10am-12:30pm and 2pm-6:30pm (Jul-Sep 10am-7pm). Closed Mon. Admission: €7.*

Begin your second day at the **place de la République**, the main square in Arles. Take in the **City Hall** (Hôtel de Ville) dating back to the 1600s. The **obelisk** with its carved features is thought to have been a trophy from the conquest of Egypt by Rome during the reign of Emperor Augustus.

On the square is the **Eglise St-Trophime/Cloître St-Trophime**. The vivid frieze of the *Last Judgment* in the doorway, a Roman sarcophagus and the cloisters are masterpieces of medieval architecture. The recently restored portal shows Christ with life-sized apostles in the columns below. *Info: place de la*

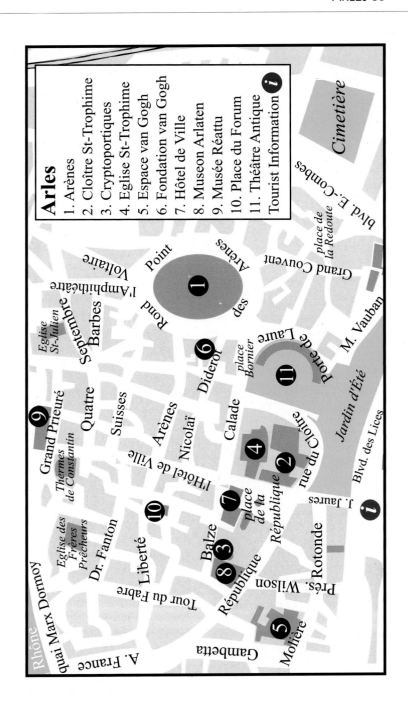

Arles
1. Arènes
2. Cloître St-Trophime
3. Cryptoportiques
4. Eglise St-Trophime
5. Espace van Gogh
6. Fondation van Gogh
7. Hôtel de Ville
8. Museon Arlaten
9. Musée Réattu
10. Place du Forum
11. Théâtre Antique
Tourist Information

SIGHTS

République. Admission: Free. €4 to the cloister.

If you want, you can visit the **Cryptoportiques**. Although, if your time is limited, skip this sight. No one is really certain of the purpose these ancient underground crypts served, which date back to 30 B.C. In World War II, they harbored the French Resistance. *Info: rue Balze. Tel. 04/90.49.36.74. Open daily 9am-noon and 2pm-6pm. Admission: €4.*

The folk culture and traditions of Arles are alive and well. At the **Museon Arlaten** (Arles Museum), women in traditional costumes watch over you as you view regional clothes, furniture, portraits and art objects. The museum has a room dedicated to Frédéric Mistral, a poet from Provence who was awarded the 1904 Nobel Prize in Literature. Since the museum is dedicated to preserving Provençal culture, the descriptions are in French and the Provençal language. *Info: 29 rue de la République. Tel. 04/90.93.58.11. Open 9:30am-noon and 2pm-6:30pm. Closed Mon (open daily Jul-Sep). Admission: €4.*

Now let's visit some of the important Roman ruins in Arles.

First, visit the **Musée de l'Arles Antique** (Museum of Ancient Arles). This modern, blue, triangular museum is located on the site of a huge Roman chariot-racing stadium (*cirque*). Mosaics, sculptures and detailed models of ancient monuments as they existed

Alternative Plan

The **Abbaye de Montmajour** is three miles (five km) northeast of Arles on route D17. The ruins of this massive Romanesque abbey sit in the middle of marshland north of Arles. You can visit the now vacant abbey and its peaceful cloister. Van Gogh came here often to paint. *Info: On route D17. Tel. 04/90.54.64.17. Open daily Apr-Sep 10am-6pm, Oct-Mar Tue-Sun 10am-5pm. Admission: €7.*

are all on view here. Most come to see the world's most famous collection of carved sarcophagi. *Info: presqu'île du Cirque Romain (1/2 mile south of the center city). Tel. 04/90.18.89.08. Open Wed-Mon 10am to 6pm. Admission: €6.*

Arles has two important Roman ruins. The **Théâtre Antique** is used today as a stage for festivals. This ancient theatre was built in the 1st century B.C. and seated 20,000. All that remains now are two columns. You can pretty much see everything by looking over the fence from rue du Cloître. *Info: rue de la Calade. Tel.*

04.90.49.36.74. Open daily May-Sep 9am-6pm, Mar, Apr and Oct 9am-11:30am and 2pm-5:30pm, Nov-Feb 10am-11:30am and 2pm-4:30pm. Admission: €4.

The highlight of your day will be a visit to the **Arènes**. It's one of the most spectacular Roman monuments in Provence. The well-preserved arena with its two tiers of arches and four medieval towers once held over 20,000 spectators. It still hosts bullfights. Some are the traditional gory type and others are "Provence style" where the bull isn't killed. *Info: Rond Point des Arènes. Tel.*

SIGHTS

04.90.49.36.74. *Open daily May-Sep 9am-6pm, Mar, Apr and Oct 9am-6pm, Nov-Feb 10am-4:30pm. Admission: €6.*

If you have time, you can squeeze in a visit to **Les Alyscamps**, one of the world's most famous cemeteries, to see Greek, Roman and Christian tombs. *Info: rue Pierre-Renaudel/avenue des Alyscamps (1/2 mile southeast from the city center). Tel. 04/90.49.36.87. Open daily 10am-11:30 and 2pm-4:30pm (until 5:30pm in the summer). Admission: €4.*

St-Rémy-de-Provence

Let's unwind in sophisticated **St-Rémy-de-Provence**. It's 12 miles (19 km) south of Avignon/15 miles (24 km) northeast of Arles.

Nostradamus, credited with predicting much of the modern era, was born here in 1503. But even he couldn't have foreseen that 500 years later so many would find this the perfect Provence town. Roman ruins are within walking distance of the mansions that grace its historic center. Its most famous resident was Vincent van Gogh, and you

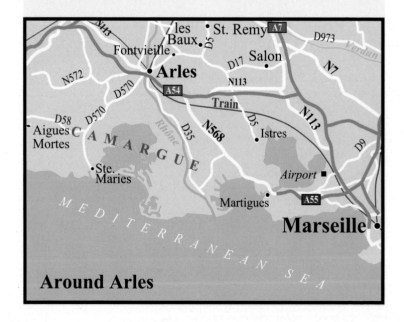

Around Arles

SIGHTS

can visit the asylum where he spent the last year of his life. But St-Rémy isn't about madness, it's about a calm and sophisticated town where you can experience the best of Provençal life. Boulevards Gambetta, Mirabeau, Marceau and Victor Hugo circle the town and are lined with cafés and boutiques. Take time to wander the maze of streets in the **Vieille Ville** (Old Town).

I recommend that you spend two days (or even more) relaxing in St-Rémy if you can. We'll discover the charming town itself first, and then we'll visit the ruins of an ancient town nearby.

The large church **Collégiale St-Martin** was rebuilt in 1820 (the original church collapsed). Frequent concerts are held featuring its 5000-pipe organ. *Info: boulevard Marceau. Open daily. Admission: Free.*

In the center of town is the **Musée Archéologique**. This museum houses a collection of Roman antiquities from the ruins of Glanum. It's located in the **Hôtel de Sade** (the family that gave us the Marquis de Sade), built in the 15th century around the remains of Roman baths. *Info: rue du Parage (center of town). Tel. 04/90.92.64.04. Open daily 11am-5pm. Admission: €3.*

Glanum

The ancient town of **Glanum** is located on route D5 in the direction of Les Baux (1/2 mile [1 km] south of St-Rémy).

The ruins here date back to the 2nd century B.C. You can

SIGHTS

de-Mausole is near Glanum off of route D5 in the direction of Les Baux.

This isolated asylum, a former monastery, still welcomes those in need of help. Its most famous patient, Vincent van Gogh, came here to spend the last year of his life after he allegedly cut off part of his left ear. During his stay, he painted such works as *Olive Trees*. You can tour the columned cloister (with a beautiful garden in the center) and the Romanesque chapel. *Info:* avenue Edgar-le-Roy (near Glanum off D5 in the direction of Les Baux). Tel. 04/90.92.77.00. Open daily Apr-Sept 9:30am-6:45pm. Open Tue-Sun Oct-Mar 10:30am-5:30pm. Admission: €4.

stroll the streets and building foundations and visit the arch (**Arc Municipal**) from the time of Julius Caesar. Across the street you'll find **Les Antiques**, two incredibly well-preserved monuments: the **Arc Triomphal** (dating from A.D. 20) and the **Mausolée** (a mausoleum dating from 30 B.C.). *Info: On D5 in the direction of Les Baux (1/2 mile [1 km] south of St-Rémy). Tel. 04/90.92.23.79. Open Tue-Sun Sep-Mar 10:30am-5pm. Open daily Apr-Aug 10am-6:30pm. Admission: €7.*

After you've visited ancient Glanum, head to another nearby sight.

The **Monastère de St-Paul-**

Les Baux-de-Provence
Perched on limestone, **Les Baux-de-Provence** is one of the most dramatic and majestic sights in Provence. It's 11 miles (18 km) northeast of Arles/18 miles (29 km) south of Avignon. It's hard to distinguish between the buildings and the rocks. The medieval town was home to one of the finest courts in medieval Provence. Abandoned in the 17th century, today it's one of

the most visited sights in France.

Les Baux gets its name from the mineral bauxite (used in the production of aluminum), which was discovered in the neighboring hills. The village is filled with galleries, boutiques and cafés operating from the stone houses. On rue Frédéric-Mistral is the **Renaissance Hôtel de Manville**. It's the Town Hall (Mairie), and you can visit its courtyard and see changing exhibits. At place St-Vincent you can take in the view, or visit the church **Eglise St-Vincent**, a museum housing works of local artist Yves Brayer, and the small **Chapelle des Pénitents** for a short concert of ancient music.

The main cobbled street is an uphill 15-minute walk. It's hard to describe the clifftop. As you walk among the ruins, you feel like you're in another world. Come here to experience a breathtaking sunset. The famous **L'Oustau de la Baumanière**, a luxury hotel complex that has been a favorite of everyone from Picasso to Elizabeth Taylor, is also here.

The walls of the ruined citadel of **Château des Baux** date from the 10th century when the first lords settled on this limestone crag. The area below is called the **Val d'Enfer** (Valley of Hell). The **Tour du Brau** still guards the entrance and houses the **Musée d'Histoire des Baux**, filled with models of the town over the ages, medieval weapons, and relics. In the small **Chapelle St-Blaise** you can watch a 10-minute film featuring olive orchards painted by van Gogh, Gauguin and Cézanne. *Info: Tel. 04/ 90.54.55.56. Open daily. Admission: €8.*

SIGHTS

At the **Cathédrale d'Images**, you can watch a state-of-the-art, 30-minute slide show in a former quarry, where 50 projectors flash images on the limestone walls. *Info: Val d'Enfer (Valley of Hell). Below Les Baux on route D27. www.cathedrale-images.com. Tel. 04/90.54.38.65. Open daily 10am-6pm. Closed Jan and Feb. Admission: €7.50.*

The Camargue

The **Camargue** – the land of French cowboys – is 9 miles (15 km) south of Arles on route D570/12 miles (19 km) east of Aigues-Mortes.

This huge (309 square miles) area is a wetlands delta where the Rhône River breaks in two before spilling into the Mediterranean Sea. It's mostly swamp, and mosquitoes are bothersome. The only people who seem to be able to tolerate the conditions are *gardiens*, cowboys who ride white horses and raise bulls here. Part of The Camargue is

filled with rice fields, cattle ranches and stud farms. The other part is a national park (**Parc Regional de Camargue**). It's home to thousands of flamingos, and is a bird-lovers paradise. The **Parc Ornithologique du Pont de Gau** is a protected area for over 400 species of birds. You can spend an entire day here exploring this national park, away from all the other tourists.

Stes-Maries-de-la-Mer

Stes-Maries-de-la-Mer is 24 miles (39 km) south of Arles/ 10 miles (18 km) south of the Camargue/80 miles (129 km) west of Marseille.

According to legend, Mary Magdalene, Mary Salome and Mary Jacobé left ancient Israel and landed in a boat here. Depending on which version you believe, they either arrived with, or were greeted and helped by, Sara, a gypsy. The town, which has a white-washed Spanish flavor to it, is a budget beach resort and very touristy. In May and October, it's loaded with Gypsies who come to the town's church as part of a pilgrimage to honor Sara.

SIGHTS

You can't miss the church **Eglise des Stes-Maries** with its large bell tower. The dark interior is filled with notes of thanks to the three Saint Marys. Note the carved boat with statues of Mary Magdalene and the Virgin Mary. The observation area has views of the town, its beaches and the Camargue. *Info: Open daily. Admission: Free. €2 (to observation area).*

There are plenty of casual and inexpensive eateries. There are also many places to ride the famous white horses that are raised here on route D570 as you enter town.

Aigues-Mortes
Not too far from Stes-Maries-de-la-Mer is another touristy, but peculiar, town. **Aigues-Mortes** is 11 miles (19 km) northwest of Stes-Maries-de-la-Mer/29 miles (48 km) south-west of Arles/ /25 miles (41 km) south of Nîmes.

France's best-preserved walled town, Aigues-Mortes means "dead waters," an appropriate name, as it's surrounded by swamp. It was once a port town and departure point for Louis IX and his crusaders bound for the Holy Land. Inside the fortress walls is a small village.

Among the many souvenir shops is the stark church **Eglise Notre-Dame des Sablons** and the attractive **place St-Louis** dominated by a statue of Louis IX. The **Tour de Constance** is a tower (complete with elevator) that affords views of The Camargue for €6.

BEST SLEEPS & EATS

SLEEPS & EATS

ARLES

Nord-Pinus €€-€€€

This famous hotel has 27 rooms and an equally famous restaurant. It's centrally located in historic Arles on the place du Forum. Antiques fill the common areas, and the rooms are interestingly decorated and well-maintained. The hotel is decorated with old

bullfighting posters (many bullfighters have stayed here), interesting black-and-white photographs of Africa by Peter Beard, and mosaics. *Info: place du Forum. www.nord-pinus.com. Tel. 04/90.93.44.44. V, MC, AE. Restaurant, bar, AC, TV, telephone.*

Hôtel de l'Amphithéâtre €

This hotel in a beautifully restored ancient building is located in the heart of the Old Town near the arena and the ancient theater. A great location for touring the main sights of Arles. Stone steps lead up to the adequate guest rooms. *Info: 5-7 rue Diderot. www.hotelamphitheatre.fr. Tel. 04/90.96.10.30. V, MC, AE. AC, TV, telephone.*

Hôtel Calendal €€

This is a bargain traveler's favorite in Arles. Located near the arena, most of its 38 basic rooms (shower in bathroom, no bathtub) are on a shaded courtyard. Rooms vary in size, so ask to see before you commit. Smaller rooms are much cheaper. Kid-friendly. *Info: 5 rue Porte de Laure. Tel. 04/90.96.11.89. www.lecalendal.com. V, MC, DC, AE. AC, TV, hairdryer.*

Brasserie Nord-Pinus €€-€€€

Wonderful and innovative French and Provençal cuisine, excellent service and beautiful surroundings (including an ancient Roman column) make this hotel restaurant a great dining experience. There's terrace dining in warm weather and a great bar (the Corrida). *Info: place du Forum. Tel. 04/90.93.44.44 or 04/90.93.02.32. Closed Feb and Wed in winter. Closed Tue, Wed (lunch) and Feb.*

La Gueule du Loup €€

French and Provençal specialties are served in this small and comfortable restaurant. It's located in a stone building near the arena. *Info: 39 rue des Arènes. Tel. 04/90.96.96.69. Closed Wed.*

LES-BAUX-DE-PROVENCE

Auberge de la Benvengudo €€-€€€

A country house that's been lovingly converted to a charming hotel one mile south of Les Baux. Surrounded by gardens, the

rooms and apartments are each beautifully decorated with antique furniture. All rooms have either a patio or balcony. The smaller rooms are a good deal. Beautiful outdoor pool. *Info: Vallon de l'Arcoule (on D78, the route to Arles). www.benvengudo.com. Tel. 04/90.54.32.54. V, MC, AE. Restaurant, outdoor pool, tennis courts, AC, TV, telephone, Wireless Internet access. Closed Nov-Feb.*

La Riboto de Taven €€-€€€

This 1835 farmhouse, outside of town in the "Valley of Hell," has been converted to an inn. The family-run restaurant and inn is known for its innovative cooking. There are six tastefully decorated rooms and apartments (located in grottos). Great outdoor pool and lovely gardens. *Info: Le Val d'Enfer (specific directions are given when you make reservations). www.riboto-de-taven.fr. Tel. 04/90.54.34.23. V, MC, AE. Restaurant, outdoor pool, AC, TV, telephone, minibar, Internet access. Closed Jan and Feb.*

La Reine Jeanne €

This small inn, located at the entrance to the village, has an attractive terrace and restaurant. There are 10 basic and clean rooms. Bathrooms have shower stalls only. *Info: grande rue Baux. www.la-reinejeanne.com. Tel. 04/90.54.32.06. V, MC. Restaurant, bar, AC, TV. Closed Jan 15-31.*

Auberge de la Benvengudo €€€

Authentic Provençal cuisine, such as *gigot d'Agneau aux pigons* (leg of lamb with pine nuts) served at this lovely country house and inn located one mile south of Les Baux. There's an impressive list of regional wines. Fixed three- course menu only. *Info: Vallon de l'Arcoule (on D78, the route to Arles). www.benvengudo.com. Tel. 04/90.54.32.54. Reservations required. Closed Sun. No lunch.*

La Riboto de Taven €€€

You'll find Provençal cooking at its best and a fine wine list at this lovely family-run restaurant and inn outside of town in the "Valley of Hell." Fixed three-course menu only. *Info: Le Val d'Enfer. www.riboto-de-taven.fr. Tel. 04/90.54.34.23. Closed Wed, Jan and Feb. No lunch. Reservations required.*

Restaurant La Reine Jeanne €€

This small inn at the entrance to the village has an attractive terrace and dining room. Stop in for panoramic views and straight-forward cooking. *Info: grande rue Baux. Tel. 04/90.54.32.06. Closed part of Jan.*

ST-RÉMY-DE-PROVENCE

Vallon de Valrugues €€-€€€

Built to look like an Italian villa, this 50-room hotel is set in a park and has all the amenities you could want. Golfers will love its putting green, there are tennis courts, and "foodies" will appreciate the fine cuisine served in the restaurant. *Info: Chemin Canto-Cigalo. www.vallondevalrugues.com.*

Tel. 04/90.92.04.40. V, MC, DC, AE. Restaurant, bar, outdoor pool, gym, TV, AC, telephone, minibar, hairdryer, safe. Closed part of Feb.

Le Mas des Carassins €€

This farmhouse (*mas*) has been nicely converted into a 14-room hotel complete with pool, restaurant and mature gardens. *Info: 1 Chemin Gaulois. www.masdescarassins.com. Tel. 04/90.92.15.48. V, MC, AE. Restaurant, outdoor pool, cable TV, minibar.*

Hôtel du Soleil €

Just a short walk from the center of town, this hotel is surrounded by gardens, has an outdoor pool and is decorated in a Provençal

theme. Rooms have small, tiled bathrooms. *Info: 35 ave. Pasteur. Tel. 04/90.92.00.63. www.hotelsoleil.com. V, MC, DC, AE. Bar, outdoor pool, TV, AC, telephone, hairdryer, safe. Closed Nov-Feb.*

Restaurant Le Provence €€-€€€

Located in the Hôtel les Ateliers de l'Image, in what once was the town's first hotel. Contemporary Provençal cuisine. *Info: 36 blvd. Victor Hugo. www.hotelphoto.com. Tel. 04/90.92.51.50. Open Thu-Mon.*

L'Assiette de Marie €-€€

An interesting dining experience in Old Town. This tiny restaurant is packed with the owner's treasures. The food is an interesting mix of Provençal, Corsican and Italian specialties. *Info: 1 rue Jaume Roux. Tel. 04/90.92.32.14. Closed Thu.*

BEST SHOPPING

St-Rémy-de-Provence
Portes Anciennes
Although known for its antique doors, this store has a good selection of antiques. Located on the outskirts of town (on the route d'Avignon). *Info: route d'Avignon. Tel. 04/90.92.13.13. Open Mon-Sat 9am-noon and 2pm-6:30pm.*

There are several other antiques stores nearby.

A popular and colorful **market** is held Wednesday mornings in and around the place de la République. Great place to find Provençal olive oil.

BEST NIGHTLIFE & ENTERTAINMENT

St-Rémy-de-Provence
Resto'bar
Located in a former movie theater. A great place to end your evening even if you're not dining at the restaurant here. *Info: 36 blvd. Victor Hugo (at L'Hôtel Les Ateliers de l'Image). Tel.04/90.92.51.50. Expensive.*

8. MARSEILLE

HIGHLIGHTS
▲ The Old Port and seafood restaurants in Marseille

▲ Sunbathing on the beach in Cassis and Bandol

▲ The fjord-like Calanques

▲ The casino and gardens of Hyères

▲ Les Gorges du Verdon

INTRO

Cosmopolitan and diverse **Marseille**, the breathtaking **Grand Canyon du Verdun**, vineyards and seafront resorts offer the traveler a little bit of everything in this area of Provence.

COORDINATES

Marseille (population 850,000) is in the south of France on the Mediterranean Sea. It's 411 miles (662km) south of Paris and 117 miles (188km) west of Nice.

Marseille was founded over 2,600 years ago, making it France's oldest city. It's also the second largest city in France. Many travelers, put off by its urban sprawl, avoid it, as most come to this part of the country for quiet villages. Those who do choose to spend time here will be rewarded, as Marseille is a vibrant, exotic (check out one of the many **Arab markets**) and cosmopolitan city.

SIGHTS

A WEEK IN & AROUND MARSEILLE

Marseille

We're going to start our day at the **Vieux Port** (Old Port).

Alternative Plan

Don't leave Marseille without trying its world-renowned *bouillabaisse*. There are two main varieties: *bouillabaisse du pêcheur* (with three types of fish) and *bouillabaisse du ravi* (with six different types of fish). Delicious! One great place known for this specialty is **Miramar** on the Old Port.

Industrial shipping has moved away from the Old Port, and now mostly pleasure boats are docked here. If arriving by car, follow the signs to *Centre-Ville* and *Vieux Port*. From the train station, Gare St-Charles, it's a 15-minute downhill walk to the port. It's dominated by two forts (**Fort St-Jean** and **Fort St-Nicolas**), and is still the heart of the city. You'll find a huge fish market here every day until early afternoon.

On the port is the ornate **Hôtel de Ville** (City Hall). If you walk uphill from City Hall, you'll be in **Le Panier** (Old Town), the oldest section of Marseille. Wander the tiny squares, cobblestone streets and stone stairways. Thankfully, after years of neglect, the Old Town is coming back to life.

At the top of Le Panier is the **Centre de la Vieille Charité** (Center of the Old Charity). This spectacular 17th-century building (a former poorhouse) houses two museums: the **Musée d'Arts Africains, Océaniens, et Amérindiens** (Museum of African, Oceanic and American Indian Art), and the **Musée d'Archéologie Mediterranéenne** (Museum of Mediterranean Archeology). *Info: 2 rue de la Charité (at the top of the Old Town). Tel. 04/91.14.58.80. Open Jun-Sep Tue-Sun 11am-6pm (Oct-May until 5pm). Closed Mon. Admission: €3 for each museum. No English information.*

Also here is the **Cathédrale de la Nouvelle Major** *(see photo at right above)*. This huge 19th-century cathedral, located in the Old Town, is neo-Byzantine (lots of marble). *Info: place de la Major (in the Old Town). Open daily. Admission: Free.*

Head back down to the Old Port.

Ferries depart from quai des Belges to **Château d'If**. This offshore island fortress was long used as a prison, and was made famous in the *Count of Monte Cristo*. *Info: Open daily. Admission: €5. Ferry ride to island: €10.*

If you're interested in shopping, head to **La Canebière**. Marseille's main boulevard begins at the Old Port and stretches through the center of the city, and it's loaded with cafés, shops of all sorts, sailors, and people of every imaginable nationality.

At number 11 is the **Musée de la Mode de Marseille**, a

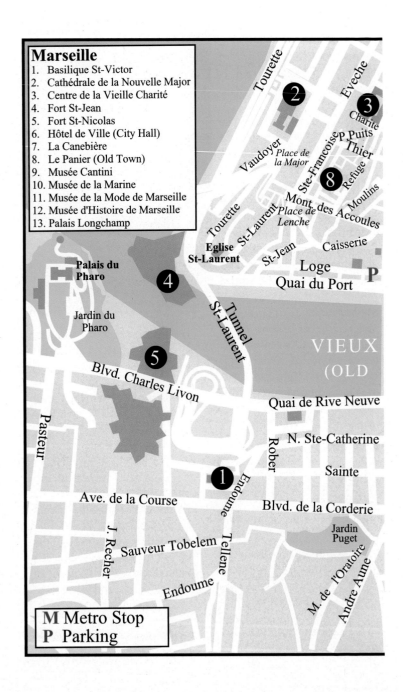

Marseille
1. Basilique St-Victor
2. Cathédrale de la Nouvelle Major
3. Centre de la Vieille Charité
4. Fort St-Jean
5. Fort St-Nicolas
6. Hôtel de Ville (City Hall)
7. La Canebière
8. Le Panier (Old Town)
9. Musée Cantini
10. Musée de la Marine
11. Musée de la Mode de Marseille
12. Musée d'Histoire de Marseille
13. Palais Longchamp

Tourette

Eveche

Charite

Vaudoyer

Place de la Major

Ste-Francoise P Puits

Thier

Refuge

Moulins

Tourette

St-Laurent

Mont des Accoules

Place de Lenche

Eglise St-Laurent

St-Jean

Caisserie

Loge

St-Laurent

Quai du Port

P

Palais du Pharo

Jardin du Pharo

Tunnel St-Laurent

VIEUX
(OLD

Blvd. Charles Livon

Quai de Rive Neuve

Pasteur

Rober

N. Ste-Catherine

Sainte

Ave. de la Course

Endoume

Blvd. de la Corderie

Jardin Puget

J. Recher

Sauveur Tobelem

Tellene

M. de l'Oratoire

Andre Aune

Endoume

M Metro Stop
P Parking

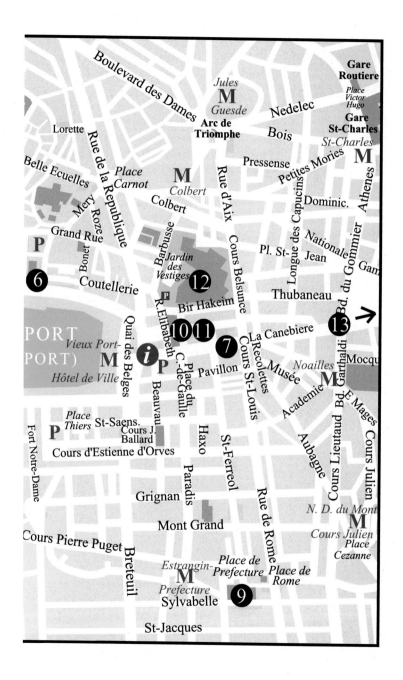

SIGHTS

fashion museum with changing exhibits. *Info: 11 La Canebière. www.espacemodemediterranee.com. Tel. 04/96.17.06.00. Open Tue-Sun 10am-5pm. Admission: €3.*

At number 7 is the **Musée de la Marine et de L'Economie de Marseille** (Marine and Economy Museum), located in a grand building housing the Chamber of Commerce. Exhibits feature the city's marine history. *Info: 7 La Canebière. Tel. 04/91.39.33.33. Open Jun-Sep Tue-Sun 11am-6pm (Oct-May until 5pm). Closed Mon. Admission: €3.*

Nearby is the **Musée d'Histoire de Marseille/Jardin des Vestiges** (Marseille History Museum/Garden of Remains). View current archeological excavations in the garden, and visit the museum to see archeological finds from ancient Marseille. *Info: Centre Bourse at rue de Bir-Hakeim. Tel. 04/91.90.42.22. Open Mon-Sat 11am-7pm. Closed Sun. Admission: €3.*

If you keep walking up La Canebière, you'll run into the **Palais Longchamp**. Built during the Second Empire, this spectacular palace won't disappoint with fountains, sculptures and columns. Both the fine-arts and natural-history museums are located here. *Info: place Bernex. Tel. 04/91.14.59.30. Closed Mon. Admission: €3.*

On the other side of the Old Port from La Panier (Old Town) are two other sights you can see if you have the time. The basilica **Basilique St-Victor** sits above a 5th-century crypt said to contain the remains of the martyr St. Cassianus. *Info: place St-Victor. Tel. 04/96.11.22.60. Open daily 9am-7pm. Admission: Free. €2 to the crypt.*

The **Musée Cantini** is a modern-art museum featuring exhibits of some of the world's up-and-coming artists. *Info: 19 rue Grignan. Tel. 04/91.54.77.75. Open Oct-May Tue-Sun 10am-5pm (Jun-Sep until 6pm). Closed Mon. Admission: €3.*

Notre-Dame de la Garde is topped by a gold statue of the Virgin Mary. This gigantic Romanesque-Byzantine basilica is 500 feet above the

SIGHTS

harbor. The elegant interior is filled with marble and mosaics, and the views outside are spectacular. *Info:* rue Fort-du-Sanctuaire (30-minute walk from harbor). Open daily 7am-7pm. Admission: Free.

Cassis, Bandol, & The Calanques

The coast of Provence offers you the choice of two relaxing port towns. First, we'll head to **Cassis**. It's 19 miles (30 km) east of Marseille/25 miles (42 km) west of Toulon.

Waterfront cafés around a beautiful port, buildings painted in pastels, boutiques and a medieval castle (the **Château de Cassis**) all make this Provence's most attractive coastal town. The water is clean and clear, and the beaches, like many others on this coast, are pebbly rather than sandy. The 1,200-foot cliff above the *château* is **Cap Canaille**, Europe's highest coastal cliff. Frankly, there isn't much to do in Cassis except lie on the beach and either look at the castle or the beachgoers, but, after all,

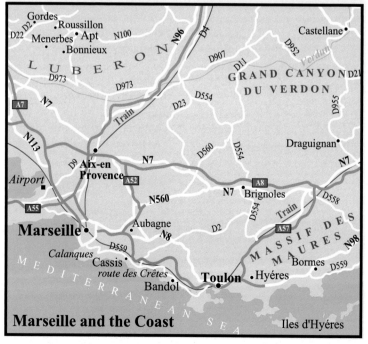

Marseille and the Coast

SIGHTS

that's what you came here for. Parking is scarce in town, so you can park outside and take a shuttle bus into town (watch for the signs saying "*navette*"). They're free and depart every 15 minutes.

Don't forget to try the aromatic white wines that are produced in the hills surrounding Cassis. There are several vineyards outside of town that offer wine tastings. One is **Domaine Ferme Blanc** on route D559, *Tel. 04/42.01.00.74.*

Between Cassis and Bandol are the **Calanques**. Like fjords,

these cliffs border the coast and hide beautiful beaches with clear blue water. You can either take a boat or hiking tour (several companies operate from the harbor in Cassis with tour prices beginning at €13) to explore the three *calanques*: **Calanque En Vau**, **Calanque Port Pin** and **Calanque Port Miou**. If you're not interested in hiking or the boat tour, the **route des Crêtes**, which heads east out of town following the signs for La Ciotat/Toulon, provides spectacular views of the coast. Note that this road is not for nervous drivers. It's very scary at points, with no guardrails protecting you from plunging straight down the cliff!

Bandol is 15 miles (24 km) southeast of Cassis/9 miles (15 km) west of Toulon. On the western end of the Côte d'Azur, this popular seaside

resort town is best known for its beaches, seaside casino, yacht-filled harbor and waterfront promenade lined with palm trees. There are 25 hotels here, and even more eating establishments. Most know the town for the wine that carries its name. The red is full-bodied and spicy, while the white is fruity, often with a hint of aniseed.

Toulon

You may find yourself in **Toulon** It's 42 miles (68 km) east of Marseille/79 miles (127 km) southwest of Cannes.

Frankly, this is really not a place you want to come on vacation. So I've given you an overview of this port city and a wonderful alternative.

Looking for sailors? Modern Toulon is the headquarters of the French Navy, and few travelers visit this busy commercial center. It's first and foremost a port town. If you visit, you'll likely head for the Old Town where you'll find the **Cathédrale Sainte-Marie** dating back to the 11th century, and the **Musée de la Marine**, a naval museum on the waterfront. *Info: Closed Tue, admission: €5.*

You can see great views of the harbor and coast from the **Tour Royale** (Royal Tower) at the east end of town near Cap Brun. You can also take in panoramas from the **corniche du Mont-Faron**, the scenic road along the slopes of Mont-Faron. Jacques Cousteau, the famous naval officer, was based in Toulon where he perfected the "aqualung,"

SIGHTS

which resulted in the growth of scuba diving here and throughout the world.

An alternative to Toulon is lovely **Brignoles** only 39 miles (70km) from Toulon, and a world away.

Wine, wine and more wine! Brignoles, on the Caramy River, is the market center for the wines of the Var region. It has a lovely Old Town, a medieval castle, a 12th-century Benedictine abbey, and former convent, the **Abbaye de La Celle**.

Many foodies flock to Brignoles to visit **Hostellerie de l'Abbaye de La Celle**, begun by famous chef Alain Ducasse, for innovative cuisine and cooking classes. *Info: South of Brignoles in La Celle. place du Général-de-Gaulle. Tel. 04/98.05.14.14. Open daily. Expensive.*

Hyères

Hyères is the oldest coastal resort along the Côte d'Azur. It's 11 miles (18 km) east of Toulon/62 miles (100 km) southeast of Aix-en-Provence. There are palm trees everywhere, and they're grown and exported from

here. Not many North American tourists vacation here, perhaps put off by the modern development along the coast. But now, visitors are rediscovering parts of the town that haven't changed since the 1930s when this was a popular European vacation destination.

The glamorous **Casino des Palmiers** is a reminder of the city's grand past. The **Vieille Ville** (Old Town) is three miles

(five km) inland on the hill and definitely worth a visit. The 12th-century **Tour St-Blaise** (St. Blaise Tower) is on triangular **place Massillon**, lined with cafés and home to a daily market. Behind the tower are narrow and steep streets lined with pastel-colored homes leading to **La Collégiale St-Paul**, an 18th-century church. The town is known for two magnificent gardens. In the southeast section of town are the **Jardins Olbius-Riquier**, tropical gardens filled with cacti and palms. Above the Old Town is the lush and lovely **parc St-Bernard** and the castle ruins.

Nearby is a medieval village worth visiting: **Bormes-les-Mimosas** is 12 miles (20 km) east of Hyères, in the hills above the coast at the western edge of the Massif des Maures.

Flowers, flowers and more flowers! Fragrant mimosas grow everywhere (thus, the name) along with other colorful flowers. There's a wonderful marked walk (**Parcours Fleuri**) that begins at the 18th-century church **Eglise St-Trophyme** and climbs up and around the ruins of the 13th-century castle. On the coast is a harbor and marina in the modern suburb of La Favière.

Iles d'Hyères
Want to get away from the mainland? The **Iles d'Hyères** are 20 miles (32 km) off the coast south of Hyères.

Boats depart from the tip of **La Tour-Fondue** (near Giens) every half-hour in the summer

(less frequently the rest of the year) for Porquerolles. Round trip fare is €16. To get to Port-Cros or Le Levant, you depart from Port d'Hyères in Hyères.

Formerly inhabited by convicts, this car-free island archipelago is mostly unspoiled with palm trees and a rocky coastline.

Porquerolles is the largest of the islands and is dotted with olive groves, vineyards and fantastic beaches. Inland, it's a hiker's and mountain biker's paradise, and a sunbather's paradise on the shore. **Le Levant** is the site of a large French Navy base. Part of the island is a nudist colony (although you must wear clothes in the village). Forested and mountainous **Port-Cros** is a national park.

Massif des Maures
The **Massif des Maures** is between route N98 (the

SIGHTS

SIGHTS

coastal road) and route A8. North from route N98 is the mountainous route D14. Hope you like hairpin turns!

It's hard to believe that this hilly, thickly wooded and sparsely populated area is so close to the frenetic coastal resorts of the western Riviera. The **Massif des Maures** stretches from Hyères to Fréjus, and much of it's inaccessible. The hills are by no means huge, but the sudden drops in the winding roads and the views make this an interesting detour from the touristy coast. There's a footpath called the GR9 for experienced hikers. "GR" stands for *Grandes Randonnées*, national hiking trails. It follows the highest ridge of the Massif des Maures.

Les Gorges du Verdon
The Grand Canyon of Verdon – **Les Gorges du Verdon** – can be visited by traveling along two cliffside roads stretching from Moustiers-Ste-Marie to Castellane. **La Corniche Sublime** (routes D19 to D71) is along the southern rim including **Pont de l'Artuby**, the highest bridge in Europe. **La route des Crêtes** (routes D952 and D23) follows the northern rim

including **Point Sublime**, the viewpoint at the entrance to the canyon. From here, the adventurous GR4 trail leads you to the bottom of the canyon, which can be reached only by foot or raft.

Hello, Gorgeous! The green waters of the Verdun River have sliced through limestone and created one of the great natural sights of not only Provence, but of France and all of Europe. This canyon is 13 miles long and as deep as 2,300 feet. At points, it's only 26 feet wide. The huge area around the canyon is a nature-lover's smorgasbord of pristine lakes, trickling streams, alpine scenery and picture-postcard villages such as **Aiguines** and **Moustiers-Ste-Marie** (*see photo below*). A drive around the canyon can take up to three hours and even longer in the summer. You'll need to fill your tank before you get to the canyon. Expect hairpin turns, along with fantastic scenery. There are many areas to stop and walk or just take in the breathtaking vistas.

BEST SLEEPS & EATS

BRIGNOLES
Hostellerie de l'Abbaye de La Celle €€€
Foodies flock to this country inn and restaurant begun by famous

chef Alain Ducasse for innovative cuisine and cooking classes. The hotel is on the site of a royal Abbey in the heart of the Coteaux Varois. The 18th-century building has ten bedrooms, each named after one of the species growing in the garden or a famous personality who stayed here. *Info: South of Brignoles in La Celle. place du Général-de-Gaulle. www.abbaye-celle.com. Tel. 04/98.05.14.14. V, MC, DC, AE. Restaurant (€€€), outdoor pool, AC, TV, telephone, CD player, minibar, in-room safe, hairdryer.*

CASSIS
Hôtel Mahogany €€
This 30-room hotel faces the Mediterranean and the coastal cliff. Nineteen of the rooms have balconies with sea views where you can enjoy breakfast which is included in the price (and later a glass of Cassis wine). Great location for a short walk into town to dine or to the beach. The friendly staff is ready to help you with reservations for dinner or local activities. *Info: Plage du Bestouan. www.hotelmahogany.com. Tel. 04/42.01.05.70. V, MC. AC (in most rooms), TV, telephone, minibar, hairdryer.*

SLEEPS & EATS

Hôtel Royal Cottage €-€€

This 25-room hotel is located on the hillside only a five-minute walk to the port (it's a steep walk back). Comfortable and clean rooms, helpful staff and a delightful outdoor swimming pool surrounded by palm trees where you can have a light lunch in the

summer. *Info: 6 ave. du 11 Novembre. www.royal-cottage.com. Tel. 04/42.01.33.34. V, MC. Outdoor pool, AC, TV, telephone, minibar, in-room safe, hairdryer, wireless Internet.*

Hôtel Laurence €

This is the budget hotel of choice in Cassis (*photo at left*). Rooms

are small, clean and some have views of the port (only two blocks away). *Info: 8 rue de l'Arène. www.cassis-hotel-laurence.com. Tel. 04/42.01.88.78. No credit cards. AC, telephone.*

Chez Nino €€-€€€

Grilled fish, *bouillabaisse* and sea urchins (the local specialty) are what you'd expect at this harborside restaurant. *Info: Quai Barthélémy (on the harbor). Tel. 04/42.01.74.32. Closed Mon, Sun (dinner) and mid-Dec to mid-Feb.*

HYÈRES
Le Petit Sejour €€

This unique two-bedroom apartment is located in a former convent within the fortress walls of the Old Town. It can accommodate up to five people, has a kitchen and a lovely, sunny terrace. *Info: 15 ter rue Fenouillet. Reservations and rates at www.lepetitsejour.com.*

MARSEILLE

Sofitel Marseille (Vieux Port) €€€

This 133-room contemporary hotel above the old port offers modern conveniences and is popular with business travelers. Good location for seeing the port's major sights. *Info: 36 blvd. Charles-Livon. Tel. 04/91.15.59.00. www.accorhotels.com. V, MC, DC, AE. Restaurant, bar, AC, TV, telephone, minibar, in-room safe, hairdryer, Internet access.*

The less expensive 110-room **Novotel (Vieux Port)** is owned by the same company, is in the same building, and shares some staff. This less expensive cousin has smaller rooms and fewer amenities, but is still a good choice. *Info: 36 blvd. Charles-Livon. Tel. 04/96.11.42.11. V, MC, DC, AE. Restaurant, bar, AC, TV, telephone, minibar, hairdryer, Internet access.*

Les Arcenaulx €€-€€€

Provençal cuisine with outdoor dining near the Old Port. You can visit the connected bookstore after your meal. *Info: 25 cours d'Estienne d'Orves. Tel. 04/91.59.80.30. Closed Sun.*

Bar de la Marine €€

On the Old Port, this bar is popular with locals for lunch. *Info: 15 quai de Rive-Neuve. Tel. 04/91.54.95.42. Open daily.*

Le Crystal €

1950s-style lounge (complete with a collection of Formica wall clocks) with a view of the Old Port. *Info: 148 quai du Port. Tel. 04/91.91.57.96. Open daily.*

MOUSTIERS-STE-MARIE

La Bastide de Moustiers €€-€€€

Remote and surrounded by lavender fields, this highly sought-

after 12-room hotel is decorated with local pottery and antiques. You can relax (or dine) at the beautiful small outdoor pool. Excellent restaurant run by chef Alain Ducasse serving innovative local and international cuisine. (€€€). *Info: Chemin de Quinson. www.bastide-moustiers.com. Tel. 04/92.70.47.47. V, MC, AE. Restaurant, bar, pool, AC, TV, telephone, minibar, hairdryer, Internet access. Closed Jan-Mar.*

Les Santons €€€

Located in a 12th-century house next to the church, this small restaurant serves hearty fare (especially game dishes) flavored with Provençal herbs. Try the interesting lavender ice cream. *Info: Place de l'Eglise in Moustiers-Ste-Marie. Tel. 04/92.74.66.48. Closed Mon (dinner), Tue and Nov-Feb.*

BEST SHOPPING

Hyères
Place Massillon in the Old Town is home to a daily market.

Marseille
There's a huge **fish market** at the Old Port on quai des Belges every day until early afternoon.

BEST NIGHTLIFE & ENTERTAINMENT

Marseille
Le Crystal
1950s-style lounge (complete with a collection of Formica wall clocks) with a view of the Old Port. *Info: 148 quai du Port. Tel.04/91.91.57.96.*

Le Trollybus
Popular dance club featuring new wave, punk rock, techno, and retro music. *Info: 22 quai de Rive Neuve. Tel. 04/91.54.30.45.*

Enigme
Popular gay bar. *Info: 22 rue Beauveau, Tel. 04/91.33.79.20.*

Opéra Municipal
Opera and classical-music concerts. *Info: 2 rue Molière. Tel. 04/91.55.11.10.*

Hyères
Try your luck at the **Casino des Palmiers** (*photo below*). *Info: 1 Avenue Ambroise Thomas. www.casinohyeres.com. Tel. 04/94 12 80 80.*

9. THE WESTERN FRENCH RIVIERA

HIGHLIGHTS

▲ A St-Tropez tan and glamorous Cannes

▲ The ancient town of Antibes

▲ The incredible clifftop village of Gourdon

▲ St-Paul-de-Vence, the most visited village in France

INTRO

The **Côte d'Azur** got its name from a guidebook written in 1887 covering the area from the Italian border to Hyères. The author was referring to the coast's clear blue skies, not, as many think, to the blue waters of the Mediterranean

Sea. Most English speakers call this area the French Riviera. Hilltop villages, art museums, coastal resorts and a St-Tropez tan all await you in the **western French Riviera**.

If you can, visit after the high-season onslaught of tourists in July and August. It's easier to drive on the *corniches* and easier to park in the small villages. The temperatures are comfortable, and life, especially in smaller towns, returns to normal. In some areas, especially seaside resorts, many places close during November and December.

Once just a quiet fishing village and favorite of artists, **St-Tropez** burst on the world scene when sexy Brigitte Bardot arrived in her

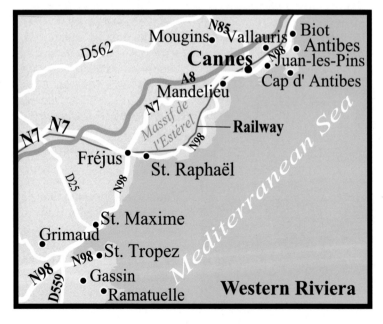

sunglasses and capri pants to star in the 1950s film *And God Created Woman*. Despite its reputation as a tourist mecca for the beautiful, rich and famous, it still retains much of its charm. Nearby, you'll find picturesque villages and great beaches in places like **Grimaud**, **Antibes**, and **Cannes**.

SIGHTS

A WEEK ON THE WESTERN FRENCH RIVIERA

St-Tropez

Let's get a tan in **St-Tropez**. It's 41 miles (66 km) northeast of Toulon/22 miles (35 km) southwest of Fréjus/47 miles (76 km) southwest of Cannes.

Come here to sit in the Old Port (**Vieux Port**) along the quai Jean-Jaurès, where yachts from all over the world dock, and enjoy some of the world's best people-watching. St-Tropez's web of narrow streets in the Old Town (**Quartier de la Ponche**) are lined with pastel-painted buildings with

red-tile roofs filled with restaurants and boutiques for every budget (especially those with an unlimited budget). You can't miss **Eglise St-Tropez**'s bell tower painted in yellow and orange (*see photo below left*). Oh, and for that St-Tropez tan, there are some great beaches here, too!

Head for the **Place des Lices** along boulevard Vasserot. Cafés shaded by plane trees line this market square. On Tuesday and Saturday mornings, it's filled with stalls selling everything from produce to antiques. In the evening, you can witness the evening promenade, where locals walk and greet each other.

There's one museum that's a must-see when you want to take a break from shopping and the beaches: The **Musée de l'Annonciade/Musée St-Tropez**. This 14th-century chapel is now a wonderful art

SIGHTS

French Riviera
(Côte d'Azur)

museum. You'll find a superb collection of Impressionist and Post-Impressionist paintings by Signac, Matisse and Dufy, to name a few. What makes this museum interesting is that many of the paintings are actually of St-Tropez. *Info: place Grammont (near the Old Port). Tel. 04/94.97.84.10. Open Jun-Sep 10am-noon and 3pm-7pm (Oct-May until 6pm). Closed Tue. Admission: €6.*

You may want to visit the **Citadelle**, where 17th-century ramparts surround this fort. Come here to take in the view of the town and coast and enjoy the quiet park. The **Musée Naval (Naval Museum)** is also here. *Info: rue de la Citadelle. Tel. 04/94.97.59.43. Closed Tue in winter. Admission: €4.*

It's the sun and beaches (*les plages*) that attract many visitors to St-Tropez. **Plage de la Bouillabaisse** (don't you love that name?) and **plage des Graniers** are closest to town, accessible by foot and popular with families.

The **Route des Plages** (Beach Road) takes you to some of the best beaches that begin 2 1/2 miles (4 km) south of town at the **plage des Salins**, accessible by bicycle or car. **Plage des Tahiti** is a favorite with nudists, and **Coco Beach** (toward Ramatuelle) is popular with gays. You'll find bars, restaurants and shops at popular and packed **plage de Pampelonne**.

A simple beach seafood restaurant? Ask one of the many celebrities that have

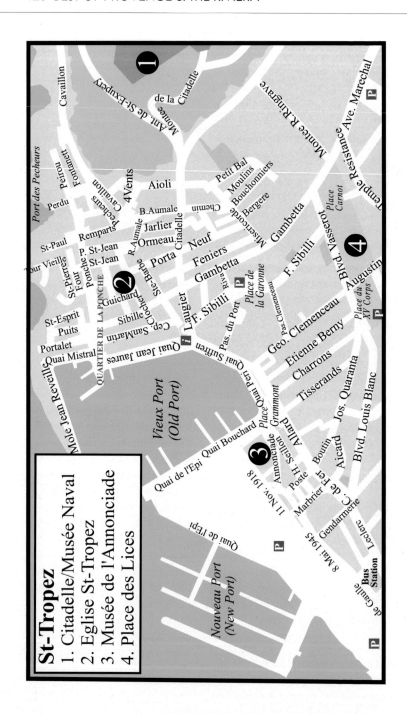

St-Tropez
1. Citadelle/Musée Naval
2. Eglise St-Tropez
3. Musée de l'Annonciade
4. Place des Lices

stopped at **Le Club 55** on place de Pampelonne. There's also a great shop selling everything you need for the beach. Alternatively, you can head ten minutes out of town to a hilltop farm for dinner at **Le Ferme du Magnan**. It's worth the drive.

Around the Gulf of St-Tropez

While St-Tropez is fabulous, don't ignore the area around it. Today we'll visit nearby gulf towns and picturesque villages (especially **Grimaud**). There's something for families, those looking for beach resorts, or those who want to spend their days on the golf course.

For families, head to **Ste-Maxime**, 7 miles (12 km) east of St-Tropez. This modern resort town directly on the Gulf of St-Tropez (across from St-Tropez) is sheltered by the Maures Mountains. The town is popular with families, and overall is much cheaper than glitzy St-Tropez. There's a large waterfront promenade and a small Old Town. You can view the **Eglise Ste-Maxime**, a 15th-century church, and the **Tour Carrée des Dames** (Dames Tower), a 16th-century tower that houses a museum dedicated to local history. Befitting a resort town, there's also a casino here. Along the casino is the **plage du Casino**. The large sandy beach **la plage de la Nartelle** is west of town.

If you're interested in visiting a picturesque village, head to **Grimaud**, 6 miles (10 km) west of St-Tropez. This picturesque village is one of France's "Villes Fleuries" (Flowered Villages) and it's truly lovely. The castle ruins (parts dating back to the 11th century) are high above the village and provide excellent vistas of St-Tropez Bay. During the day the town is filled with tourists, but at night it's a quiet place to dine and stroll. The car-free town of **Port Grimaud** on the coast was constructed in the 1960s as a private resort complete with canals. Sort of a 1960s Venice in the South of France.

SIGHTS

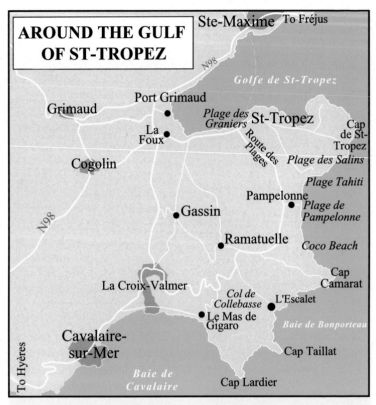

AROUND THE GULF OF ST-TROPEZ

Ste-Maxime To Fréjus

N98

Golfe de St-Tropez

Grimaud Port Grimaud

Plage des Graniers St-Tropez

Cap de St-Tropez

La Foux

Route des Plages

Plage des Salins

Cogolin

Plage Tahiti

Pampelonne Plage de Pampelonne

N98 Gassin

Ramatuelle Coco Beach

La Croix-Valmer

Cap Camarat

Col de Collebasse L'Escalet

Le Mas de Gigaro

Baie de Bonporteau

Cavalaire-sur-Mer

Cap Taillat

To Hyères

Baie de Cavalaire Cap Lardier

Lovely Grimaud has some quaint places to dine on the lovely place des Pénitents (*see Best Sleeps & Eats section for details*).

For great views of the Bay of Pampelonne, head to **Ramatuelle**, 7 miles (12km) southwest of St-Tropez. Ramatuelle is built into the hills above the Bay of Pampelonne. It's surrounded by vineyards, and the village is enclosed by ramparts.

Ancient stone houses line the narrow streets filled with boutiques and souvenir shops for the many day-trippers from St-Tropez. Lots of restaurants and small hotels.

Four miles (seven km) north of Ramatuelle is **Gassin**, another village worth a visit. Gassin is perched high up on a rock surrounded by vineyards. It's less commercial than nearby Ramatuelle. The village has ancient homes and

winding streets. Its location is really the reason to visit. Not only can you see the Gulf of St-Tropez, but on a clear day, your view extends over the Maures Mountains.

If beach resorts are more to your liking, the area around the Gulf of St-Tropez offers many opportunities. **Fréjus** is 20 miles (34 km) northeast of St-Tropez. Fréjus and nearby St-Raphaël seem to blend into each other as commercial beach resorts. Despite the town's bikini-wearing image, Fréjus's **Old Town** (Vieille Ville) has important Roman sights. The town was founded in 49 B.C. by Julius Caesar. You can view the remains of the **Théâtre Antique**, the 12,000-seat **Arènes** (an arena used today for the occasional bullfight and concert), and remaining arches of an **aqueduct**. Take a break from your tanning and visit these ruins.

Cité Épiscopale is an impressive fortified group of religious buildings in the Old Town. Outside the entry to the 12th-century cathedral is an octagonal baptistery from a 5th-century church that was located here. The cloisters feature galleries decorated with paintings from the 14th century. There's also a small archeology museum of Roman finds from the surrounding area. *Info: 58 rue de Fleury (in the Old Town). Tel. 04/94.51.26.30. Cloister, baptistery and museum are open Apr-Sep daily 9am-6pm. Oct-Mar Tue-Sun 9am-noon and 2pm-5pm. Cathedral is open daily 8:30am-noon and 2pm-6pm. Admission: Free (cathedral). Cloister, baptistery and museum: €5.*

Merging with Fréjus, **St-Raphaël** (1/2 mile [one km] southeast of Fréjus) is a modern beach resort. Unlike its neighbor, it has few historic sights. The **Old Town** (Vieille Ville) is the site of two churches, the 19th-century **Notre-Dame de la Victoire** and the 12th-century **Eglise des Templiers**. Beside the Eglise des Templiers is the **Musée d'Archéologie Sous-Marine**, a museum dedicated to

SIGHTS

underwater archeology (*closed Sun and Mon, admission: €4*). You'll find a casino, hotels, and a promenade along the seafront. There are also five golf courses near St-Raphaël.

First and foremost, this town is a beach town. Closest to town is **plage du Veillat**. A five-minute walk east of town is **plage Beau Rivage**. Even further east (about five miles) is **plage du Débarquement**. It was at this beach that the Allies landed in August of 1944 to begin their quest to liberate occupied France in World War II. In the other direction, about six miles west of town, is **plage de St-Ayguls**, a nude beach.

For stunning scenery, drive through the **Massif de l'Estérel** (*see photo below*) from St-Raphaël to La Napoule. This barren area of red volcanic rock provides strange and dramatic views. You can either travel north on route N7 or (for the more adventurous) along the coast on the **Corniche de l'Estérel** (route N98).

Looking for golf courses? Then visit **Mandelieu/La Napoule-Plage**. It's 5 miles (8 km) southwest of Cannes/20 miles (32 km) northeast of St-Raphaël. La Napoule is surrounded by the large resort town of Mandelieu. It was once a small fishing village on the Golfe de la Napoule.

Its main sight is its *château*, a 14th-century fortress on the port. It was converted to a strange and interesting castle by eccentric American sculptor Henry Clews in the early 1900s. Now it's a museum of his works. *Info: Tel. 04/93.49.95.05. Three guided tours daily, admission: €6.*

Cannes

Get glamorous in **Cannes**. It's 20 miles (33 km) southwest of Nice/45 miles (73 km) northeast of St-Tropez.

This alluring resort with nearly perfect weather is best known for its **international film festival** (Festival International du Film) held every May, hosting countless film stars, over 4,000 journalists, and 1,500 other members of the media from around the world.

Head to **La Croisette**, a two-mile promenade on the waterfront. You'll see palm trees, polished yachts from every imaginable place in the world, incredible shops, ultra-luxury hotels and some of the most interesting sun-worshippers in the world.

At the beginning of La Croisette is the **Palais des Festivals** (Festivals Palace)/**Allée des Etoiles** (Walk of the Stars). Nicknamed "the bunker," the modern Palais des Festivals is the venue for the International Film Festival and many other events. Over 300 handprints are set in concrete on the Walk of Stars surrounding the Festival Hall. Also here is the Casino Croisette.

At number 47 La Croisette is **Malmaison**. This 19th-century mansion hosts changing photography and modern-art exhibits. *Info: 47 La Croisette. Tel. 04/93.06.44.90. Closed Mon. Admission: Depends on the exhibit.*

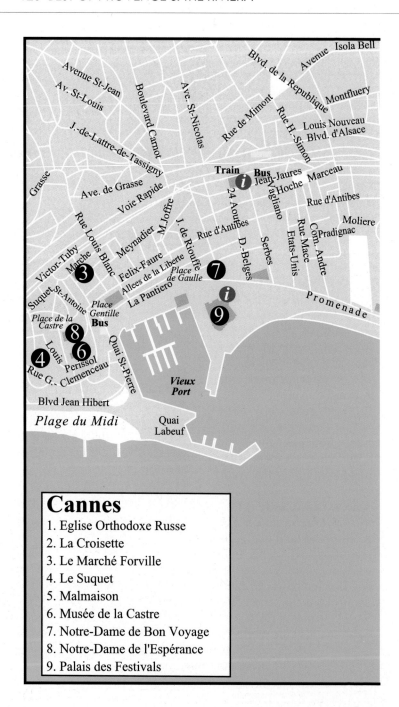

Cannes

1. Eglise Orthodoxe Russe
2. La Croisette
3. Le Marché Forville
4. Le Suquet
5. Malmaison
6. Musée de la Castre
7. Notre-Dame de Bon Voyage
8. Notre-Dame de l'Espérance
9. Palais des Festivals

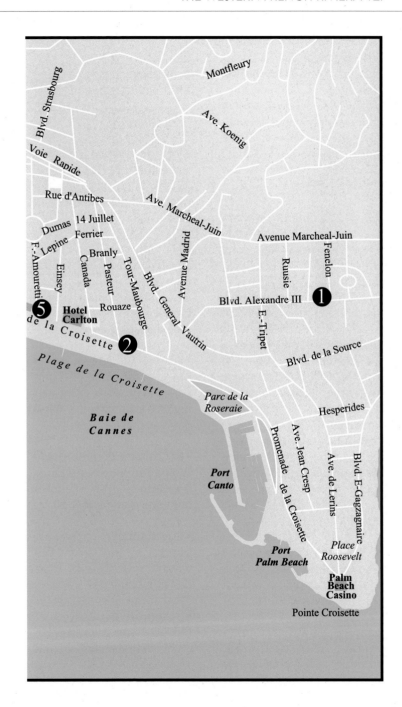

Montfleury

Blvd. Strasbourg

Ave. Koenig

Voie Rapide

Rue d'Antibes

Ave. Marcheal-Juin

Avenue Marcheal-Juin

Dumas 14 Juillet
Ferrier
F.-Amouretti
Lepine
Einsey
Canada
Branly
Pasteur
Tour-Maubourge
Avenue Madrid
Blvd. General Vautrin
Russie
Fenelon

①

Blvd. Alexandre III

E. Tripet

⑤ **Hotel Carlton**

Rouaze

de la Croisette

②

Blvd. de la Source

Plage de la Croisette

Parc de la Roseraie

Hesperides

Baie de Cannes

Port Canto

Promenade de la Croisette

Ave. Jean Cresp

Ave. de Lerins

Blvd. E-Gagzagnaire

Port Palm Beach

Place Roosevelt

Palm Beach Casino

Pointe Croisette

SIGHTS

Just north of the Festivals Palace is **Notre-Dame de Bon Voyage**, a 19th-century Gothic-style church, where you can pray that you won't lose all your money at the nearby casinos. *Info: Square Mérimée. Open daily. Admission: Free.*

If you're looking for a place to take a break, there are plenty of cafés and restaurants along the waterfront.

The **Old Town** (Le Suquet) is on a hill on the west end of town. Narrow passageways lead to the **Tour du Suquet**, a 14th-century tower. *Info: Up rue St-Antoine from the waterfront (above quai St-Pierre).*

In the Old Town on the place de la Castre is **Notre-Dame de l'Espérance**, a 16th-century Gothic church. *Info: place de la Castre. Open daily. Admission: Free.*

At the top of Old Town is the **Musée de la Castre**. This museum is ambitious. It has a section on Mediterranean antiquities, a section of 19th-century paintings, and a section with sculpture, paintings and decorative arts from all over the world. *Info: In the Château de la Castre at the top of La Suquet. Tel. 04/93.38.55.26. Closed Tue. Admission: €4.*

If you're into shopping, there's something for everyone here. A few highlights of the phenomenal shopping in Cannes are:

• **Le Marché Forville**: a covered market not too far from Festival Hall featuring a flea market (Mon) and a produce and flower market (Tue through Sun)

• **Galeries Lafayette**: a branch of this upscale French department store is located near the train station at 6 rue du Maréchal-Foch

• **La Croisette**: the promenade is loaded with designer boutiques (the Chanel boutique is at number 5!)

• **Rue d'Antibes**: a street (two blocks inland from the waterfront) filled with designer boutiques

• **Cannolive**: Provençal products, especially olive oils, at this long-standing shop at 16 rue Vénizelos

• **Rue Meynadier**: inland from the port, this pedestrian-only street is loaded with shops for most budgets

While walking around town, you may stumble upon **Eglise Orthodoxe Russe**. It's so strange to see a Russian Orthodox Church in the South of France. The church, complete with onion dome, is dedicated to Michael the Archangel and was built by an expatriate Russian in the late 1800s. *Info: 30 boulevard Alexandre III. Open for services only. Admission: Free.*

Ready to take a break or just be a voyeur? Head to the beach! The **Plage de la Croisette** is along the promenade of the same name.

For the most part, this is not a public beach. You must pay a

fee (beginning at about €15) for use of a chaise longue, access to showers, food and drink service, an umbrella, and other amenities.

For free beaches, try **plage Gazagnaire** to the east, or **plage du Midi** to the west.

Off the coast of Cannes are the **Iles de Lérins**. Traffic-free and tranquil, these islands can be reached by ferry from the Old Port (€10). It takes 15 minutes to get to **Ile Ste-Marguerite** (filled with pine and eucalyptus trees, it's home to Fort Royal, where "The Man in the Iron Mask" was imprisoned); and 30 minutes to **Ile St-Honorat** (home to a fortified abbey).

Golfers flock to the area around Cannes. Five miles (eight km) northeast of Cannes on route D35 is the **Golf Club de Cannes-Mandelieu**, where golfers can enjoy two stunning golf courses (18 holes and 9 holes). *Info:*

Alternate Plan

If you're interested in abstract art, you can visit the **Espace de l'Art Concret** outside of Cannes isn Mouans-Sartoux (in the castle), which houses a collection of 350 abstract works. *Info: Tel. 04/93.75.71.50. Closed Mon-Tue in winter. Admission: €5.*

SIGHTS

www.golfoldcourse.com. Tel. 04/92.97.32.00. Open daily.

Around Cannes

The area around Cannes offers local-history museums, photography museums, art museums, and perfume museums. You can seek these out on this day plan.

We'll start in **Mougins**, five miles (eight km) north of Cannes. The area around Mougins has become a business center and home to thousands of French and international companies. The old village has been restored, and is filled with flowers and galleries. There's a free **Museum of Local History** in the St-Bernardin Chapel (*Tel. 04/92.92.50.42*) and a **Museum of Photography** (see below). Picasso and other artists came here in the 1960s, and Picasso died here in 1973. His final home is in the priory next door to the **Chapelle Notre-Dame de Vie**, an ancient church overlooking the Bay of Cannes. Note that Picasso's former home is privately owned, and the chapel is only open for services. *Info: It's located off of route D35 (1 mile [1.5 km] southeast of town).*

Alternate Plan

At the Aire des Bréguières (a rest stop along route A8, three miles [five km] south of town) is the **Musée de l'Automobiliste**. Over 100 vintage automobiles are showcased in this modern facility. *Info: Tel. 04/93.69.27.80. Open daily. Closed Nov. Admission: €8.*

Behind the Porte Sarassine, a 12th-century gate, the **Musée de la Photographie** is filled with photography equipment and photos (some of Picasso during his life in Mougins). *Info: At the Porte Sarassine 67 rue de l'Eglise. Tel. 04/93.75.85.67. Open daily. Admission: €5.*

Next head to **Grasse**. It's 10 miles (17 km) northwest of Cannes/14 miles (22 km) northwest of Antibes/26 miles (42 km) southwest of Nice. Once a famous resort destination (the likes of Queen Victoria used to come here), today Grasse is a modern town and the headquarters of some of the world's best-known and largest perfume manufacturers. The majority of all perfume sold in the world contains essences from Grasse. The

city's three largest perfume makers have free guided tours: **Fragonard** at 20 boulevard Fragonard (*photo above*), **Molinard** at 60 boulevard Victor-Hugo, and **Galimard** at 73 route de Cannes (two miles [three km] south of the center of town). Lots of signs point the way to these factories. The **Vieille Ville** (Old Town) has narrow, steep streets without the glitz of coastal old towns.

Grasse has three very different museums. The **Musée International de la Parfumerie** (International Perfume Museum) will tell you everything you wanted to know about perfume and its 4,000-year history. Put your nose to the test at one exhibit by trying to identify different fragrances. *Info: 8 place du Cours. Tel. 04/93.36.80.20. Closed Mon and Tue in winter. Admission: €4.*

Another museum is the **Musée Fragonard**. Fragonard was one of France's distinguished 18th-century artists. This museum honors this native son of Grasse and showcases his paintings. *Info: 23 boulevard Fragonard. Tel. 04/93.36.02.71. Closed Tue in winter. Admission: €4.*

You'll find local paintings, archeological finds, household

SIGHTS

items and pottery at the **Musée d'Art et d'Histoire de Provence** (Museum of Art and History of Provence). *Info: 2 rue Mirabeau. Tel. 04/ 93.36.01.61. Closed Tue in winter. Admission: Free.*

If you're up for more touring, you can visit **Vallauris/Golfe-Juan**. It's four miles (six km) west of Antibes/four miles (six km) northeast of Cannes.

Vallauris is a working-class-town and has long been a center for the production of **pottery and ceramics**. Most come here to visit the museum dedicated to the works of Picasso. On the coast is the port of Golfe-Juan. It was here

in 1815 that Napoléon arrived after being exiled to the island of Elba in his attempt to return to power. Today it's a family beach resort.

Picasso lived in this town in the 1940s and devoted much of his time to creating pottery. The **Musée National Picasso** (La Guerre et La Paix) is located in the 16th-century **Château de Vallauris**. Two of Picasso's paintings (*La Paix* [Peace] and *La Guerre* [War]) decorate three of the walls. Also here are the **Musée de la Céramique Moderne**, exhibiting Picasso and others' ceramic works, and **Musée Magnelli**, devoted to the works of Italian abstract artist Alberto Magnelli. *Info: place de la Libération. Tel. 04/ 93.64.71.83. Closed Tue. Admission: €4.*

If you'd like to take a detour from the coast and its resorts, you can drive 110 miles (176 km) along the **Route Napoléon** from Grasse (near the coast) to Sisteron, mainly on route N85. Napoléon Bonaparte abdicated in April, 1814, and fled to the island of Elba. Nearly a year later, he landed near Cannes. From Cannes, Napoléon and 1,200 men followed small trails and mule tracks through the hills. Traveling its entirety can take up to 15 hours.

Plaques commemorating his return are found all along this panoramic drive. Sisteron is the northern gateway to Provence. It's crowned by a 14th-century fortified citadel. On your way up to the citadel is the 12th-century church of **Notre-Dame des Pommiers**. You'll find incredible views of the Durance River valley from the citadel after you climb up Sisteron's tiny winding streets, covered alleys and steep stairways. The last inhabitants of the citadel were the Nazis in 1944, who used it as a prison and military base.

Antibes

Antibes is an ancient town with 17th-century ramparts and a fortress wall dropping into the sea. It's 9 miles (15 km) southeast of Nice/7 miles (11 km) northeast of Cannes. The streets of its **Old Town** (Vieil Antibes) are lined with Italianate buildings with red-tile roofs. High over the water is the medieval castle, the **Château Grimaldi**. It's also a major tourist destination, with

a sandy beach, boutiques and cafés. **Port Vauban Harbor** is packed with some of the largest yachts in the world.

Begin your day in Antibes at the harborside car park along avenue de Verdun (the main street along the harbor).

Pass through the arched gateway (the **Porte Marine**). The rampart walls date back to the 17th century when Antibes was the last town before the Italian border. You'll now be in the Old Town (**Vieil Antibes**) on rue Aubernon lined with Italianate buildings.

If you're looking to take a break at a café, head to the tree-lined **Place Nationale** on rue de la République.

The heart of Antibes is the 19th-century canopy of the **Marché Provençal** (Provence Market). Everything from

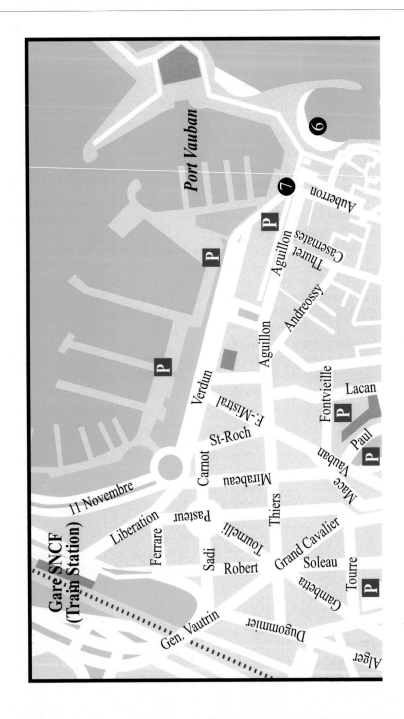

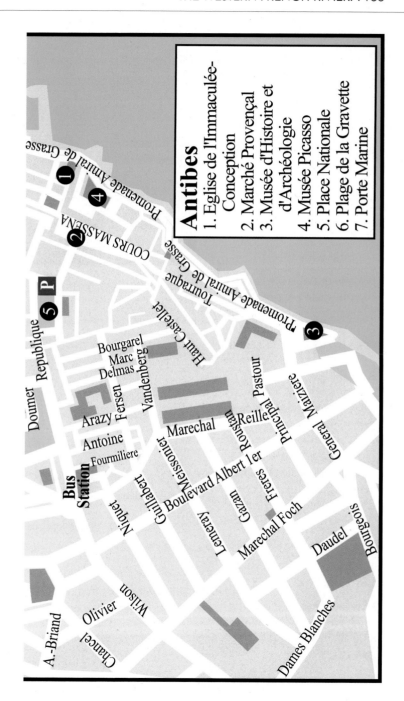

Antibes
1. Eglise de l'Immaculée-Conception
2. Marché Provençal
3. Musée d'Histoire et d'Archéologie
4. Musée Picasso
5. Place Nationale
6. Plage de la Gravette
7. Porte Marine

SIGHTS

flowers to produce to crafts to beachwear can be found here.

Regional products are sold at **Balade en Provence**, a small shop along the covered market. You should go downstairs where there is a good selection of regional wines, absinthe, and a tasting room. *Info: 25 cours Massena. Tel. 04/93.34.93.00.*

In the Old Town, at place de la Cathédrale, is the **Eglise de l'Immaculée-Conception** (Church of the Immaculate Conception). Its bell tower dates back to the 11th century. Inside you can view its Baroque painted altars.

Across the street from the cathedral is the famous **Musée Picasso**. Picasso spent a very productive year here in the early 1940s at the Château Grimaldi. He gave the museum 300 works (ceramics, drawings, paintings, lithographs, tapestries,

Alternate Plan 🚶

Whales, sharks, dolphins, sea lions, waterslides, miniature golf, petting zoo...you get the picture. Children will love **Marineland**. *Info: On route N7 2 miles (4 km) east of town. Tel. 04/93.33.49.49. Closed Oct-Jan but otherwise open daily. Admission: €36 adults, €28 children.*

sculptures, and oils on paper). There are works by other artists, too, including Miró and Calder. *Info: place du Château (in the Château Grimaldi). Tel. 04/92.90.54.20. Open mid-Sep to mid-June 10am-noon and 2pm-6pm, mid-June to mid-Sep 10am-6pm. Admission: €6.*

If you're interested in catching some rays, join the sunbathers at the public beach, **plage de la Gravette**.

The archeology museum **Musée d'Histoire et d'Archéologie** is located in the fortress Bastion-St-André. It's filled with finds from the area dating back to the Greeks, who settled here in the 4th-century B.C. *Info: Tel. 04/92.90.53.31. Open Tue-Sun 10am-noon*

and 2pm-6pm. *Closed Mon. Admission: €3.*

You may want to spend some time in **Cap d' Antibes**, just one mile (two km) south of Antibes. Since the 19th century, this peninsula has been home to luxury villas shaded by massive pines and protected by privacy gates.

One of the world's most glamorous hotels (**Hôtel du Cap-Eden Roc**) is located here. There are fabulous views from the lighthouse (**Phare de la Garoupe**) next to the 16th-century chapel of **Notre-Dame-de-la-Garoupe**.

If you're interested in history, you can visit a museum devoted to Napoleon.

Located in a 17th –century fort and tower, the **Musée Naval et Napoléonien** has a collection of Napoleonic memorabilia (he wore lots of hats). You can climb the tower for great views of the coast. *Info: boulevard J.-F.-Kennedy. Tel. 04/93.61.45.32. Closed Sun and Mon. Admission: €3.*

If you're interested in subtropical plants and trees, head to the **Jardin Thuret**.

Thuret was the man responsible for introducing the palm tree to this area. *Info: boulevard du Cap. Tel. 04/93.67.88.00. Closed weekends. Admission: Free.*

A Memorable Sunset
Begin this phenomenal walk at the plage de la Garoupe, the cape's beach. You can park at the public parking lot. At the end of the beach and parking lot is the Sentier du Littoral. This stone path (at times dirt) has steps etched into the rocky coastline. Although it winds its way around the entire cape, remember that you need to return to your car. It's for the adventurous and at times the waves can make the path slippery and dangerous. A memorable walk at sunset!

SIGHTS

For dinner (or better yet, after dinner), you may want to visit **Juan-les-Pins**. It's three miles (five km) southwest of Antibes.

Modern, crowded, sexy and a little bit naughty. Juan-les-Pins, developed in the 1920s, is known for its nightlife and tends to draw a younger crowd than nearby Antibes. You can take a break from visiting the clubs at **Eden Casino**. While most of the coast has pebble beaches, the town's three public beaches, **plage de Juan-les-Pins**, **plage de la Salis** and **plage de la Garoupe**, are sandy. It hosts a world-renowned jazz festival every July. *Info: www.antibes-juanlespins.com.*

Around Antibes
Pottery, art and unbelievable scenery are in store for you on this day plan in the area around Antibes. Begin in **Biot**, four miles (six km) northwest of Antibes. This 16th-century hilltop village is known for its pottery, ceramics and glassblowing. Around the main square, the **place des Arcades**, are the ancient gateways and the **Eglise de Biot** with its elaborately decorated 15th-century altar screens.

There are many shops here where you can buy pottery, ceramics and decorative glassware, and most of them are near the place des Arcades. You can watch glassblowers and purchase expensive glassware at **Verreries de Biot** at 5 chemin des Combes on the edge of town.

The **Musée d'Histoire Locale et de Céramique Biotoise** chronicles the importance of ceramics, pottery and glassblowing in local history. *Info: place de la Chapelle/9 rue St-Sébastien. Tel. 04/93.65.54.54. Closed Mon and Tue. Admission: €3.*

You may also want to visit the **Musée National Fernand-Léger** on the east end of the village. Léger was a French cubist painter who died in 1955. This national museum, with its very colorful exterior, houses over 300 of his works. *Info: Chemin du Val de Pome (on the east end of the village). Tel. 04/92.91.50.30. Closed Tue. Admission: €5.50.*

Next door to the Musée National Fernand-Léger is the **Bonsaï Arboretum** with a collection of over 1,000 bonsai trees, some of which

are over 1,000 years old. *Info: 229 chemin du Val de Pome (on the east end of the village). Tel. 04/93.65.63.99. Closed Tue. Admission: €4.*

Inland is the incredible village of **Gourdon**, 9 miles (14 km) north of Grasse.

This clifftop village stands dramatically on limestone overlooking the Loup River Valley. It's worth the drive up the winding roads. The town offers spectacular views (and I do mean spectacular) of both the coast and the river canyon. The Loup River has cut its way through the limestone to create a series of rapids and waterfalls, and the river canyon is one of the most accessible in the area. You can walk from town down the adventurous **chemin du Paradis**. The city is popular with hikers, rafters and trout fishermen. It's an ancient feudal town where you can visit the **Gourdon Castle**, which houses a museum with 16th- and 17th-century paintings, ancient weapons and armor. *Info: Tel. 04/ 93.09.68.02. Open daily Jun-Sep 11am-1pm and 2pm-7pm, Oct-May Wed-Sun 2pm-6pm. Admission: €4.*

Even if you don't dine here, check out the spectacular setting of the restaurant **Le Nid d'Aigle**, on a terrace perched on the edge of a hill.

If you want to check out one more village near Antibes, head to the lovely town of **Tourrettes-sur-Loup**. It's 18 miles (29 km) west of Nice/4 miles (6 km) west of Vence.

This village with its three towers sits on a cliff overlooking the Loup River Valley. The walls of the outer buildings of the village also serve as ramparts. It's a center for the cultivation of violets, and you'll see them everywhere. The **Old Town** is lovely and worth a stroll. You can visit the **Chapelle St-Jean** next to **Roman ruins**. The town is loaded with interesting galleries selling their crafts and plenty of candy shops, some of them selling sugar candy made with local violets (I told you they were everywhere).

Further Afield
Join the crowds in **St-Paul-de-Vence**, 19 miles (31 km) north

of Nice. Said to be the most visited village in France, St-Paul is crowded with day-trippers from the coastal resort towns and Nice. What makes it so popular is its walled, beautifully preserved **Old Town** of stone houses dating back to the 16th and 17th centuries. You can walk down the car-free main street (**Grande Rue**) past its souvenir shops and art galleries, up to the art-filled **La Collégiale de la Conversion de St-Paul** (an early Gothic church), and visit the **Musée d'Histoire Locale** (Local History Museum).

Outside the town walls on the hilltop (a 15-minute uphill walk from town or access by car) is the **Fondation Maeght**. Even those not interested in modern art can appreciate this world-famous venue. Glass walls let you take in the pine-shaded gardens and terraces while you view changing exhibits of works by such artists as Chagall, Matisse, Kandinsky, Calder, and Miró. This private museum was established in the 1960s by art dealer Aimé Maeght, and its unique architecture alone is worth a visit. *Info: Outside the town walls on the hilltop (a 15-minute uphill walk from* town or access by car). *www.fondation-maeght.com. Tel. 04/93.32.81.63. Open daily July-Sep 10am-7pm. Oct-June 10am-6pm. Admission: €11.*

You don't have to go to the Fondation Maeght to see famous art. **La Colombe d'Or** is located in an inn of the same name. It has works of such notables as Picasso and Utrillo on the walls. The restaurant and bar were favorites of these then-struggling artists who paid their bills with their art. Although the food is expensive and you can get better elsewhere, where else can you dine among such art? *Info: 1 place du Général-de-Gaulle. Tel. 04/93.32.80.02. Closed Nov and Dec. Expensive.*

Just two miles (four km) north of St-Paul-de-Vence is the city of **Vence**.

Vence is a modern commercial town and most travelers head to its walled **Old Town** (Cité Historique). Most of the renovated Old Town dates back to the 15th century. Sections of the original walls survive and there are five gates (*portes*) that remain. Inside these gates are the 13th-century

watchtower of the **Château de Villeneuve** on **place du Frêne** (which takes its name from the ancient ash tree (*frêne*) here), the **place du Peyra** (with its lovely fountains), and the **place Clemenceau** (dominated by the City Hall). On **place Godeau** is the **Cathédrale de la Nativité de la Vierge** (Cathedral of the Birth of the Virgin), with portions dating back to the 10th century.

On the northern outskirts of town is the **Chapelle du Rosaire** (Chapel of the Rosary). At the age of 77, in thanks to a Dominican nun (and sometimes model!) who nursed him back to health, Matisse designed and decorated this small chapel on the northern outskirts of town. Its white walls are highlighted with blue-and-green stained-glass windows and black-and-white Stations of the Cross. The admission includes entry to **L'Espace Matisse**, a museum that chronicles the design and construction of the chapel. *Info: 466 avenue Henri-Matisse. Tel. 04/93.58.03.26. Open Tue and Thu 10am-11:30am and 2pm-5:30pm. Closed mid-Nov to mid-Dec. Admission: €3.*

SIGHTS

If you're up for more touring today, you can visit **Cagnes-sur-Mer**, 4 miles (6 km) south of St-Paul-de-Vence/13 miles (21 km) northeast of Cannes.

Cagnes-sur-Mer is really three different places. At the sea is the former fishing village and now modern beach resort of **Cros-de-Cagnes** (with a pebble beach). Inland is the modern town of **Cagnes-Ville**, and up the hill is the beautiful fortified medieval village of **Haut-de-Cagnes** (*photo below*).

In Haut-de-Cagnes, you'll find the **Château de Cagne**. This Grimaldi fortress was built in the early 1300s. Inside its walls is an elegant palace dating back to 1602. It houses the museum of modern Mediterranean art, a museum dedicated to the history of the olive tree, and a collection of portraits by 1930s French singer Suzy Solidor (who?). *Info: place Grimaldi. Tel. 04/ 93.02.47.30. Closed Tue. Admission: €3.*

Admirers of Renoir should visit the **Musée Renoir**, located in the former home of the artist. It has been renovated and restored to how it was when he died in 1919. The museum sits in the middle of olive groves just east of the Old Town. Eleven of his paintings and the largest collection of his sculpture are here, along with those of his contemporaries. *Info: avenue*

des Collettes (brown signs mark the way). Tel. 04/93.20.61.07. Open Oct-Apr Wed-Mon 10am-11:30am and 2pm-5pm (May-Sep until 6pm). Closed Tue. Admission: €4.

BEST SLEEPS & EATS

ANTIBES/CAP D'ANTIBES

Hôtel du Cap-Eden Roc €€€
Simply one of the world's most glamorous hotels. It's so exclusive that it doesn't take credit cards. The swimming pool, dug into solid rock, is spectacular. *Info: Blvd. J.F.-Kennedy in Cap d'Antibes.*

www.edenroc-hotel.fr. Tel. 04/93.61.39.01. Restaurant, bar, outdor pool, tennis courts, AC, TV, telephone, minibar, safe, hairdryer, Internet access.

Castel Garoupe €€
This hotel is located in a villa in Cap d'Antibes. Attractive pool, flowered gardens and comfortable rooms. *Info: 959 blvd. de la Garoupe. www.castel-garoupe.com. Tel. 04/93.61.36.51. V, MC, AE. Bar, outdoor pool, gym, AC (some rooms), TV (some rooms), telephone, minibar, safe, hairdryer.*

Hôtel La Jabotte €-€€
A small gem of a hotel (really more like a bed and breakfast) for the cost, hidden down an alley in Cap d'Antibes. Lovely patio garden, basic accommodations and friendly owners (and their ever-present dog). *Info: 13*

ave. Max-Maurey. www.jabotte.com. Tel. 04/93.61.45.89. V, MC. Telephone. WiFi available.

Les Vieux Murs €€€

This restaurant/tavern is located in a vaulted room inside the town walls near the Musée Picasso. Local seafood is the specialty. *Info: 25 promenade Amiral-de-Grasse. www.lesvieuxmurs.com. Tel. 04/93.34.06.73. Closed Mon and Tue (lunch).*

Le Brûlot €-€€

Crowded, hectic bistro one street inland from the open-air market, serving authentic Provençal fare and pizza cooked in a wood oven. *Info: 3 rue Frédéric-Isnard (off of rue Clemenceau). Tel. 04/93.34.17.76. Closed Sun. No lunch Mon-Wed.*

CANNES

InterContinental Carlton €€€

The hotel in Cannes (and has been for years). Fashionable, plush and filled with celebrities during the film festival. Scenes from the

Cary Grant and Grace Kelly movie *To Catch a Thief* were filmed here. Every amenity imaginable. Fantastic waterfront location with its own private beach. *Info: 58 blvd. De la Croisette. www.ichotelsgroup.com. Tel. 04/93.06.40.06. V, MC, DC, AE. Restaurant, bar, gym, room service,* AC, TV, telephone, CD player, minibar, in-room safe, hairdryer.

Hôtel Splendid €€-€€€

We can't all stay at the Carlton, but we can perhaps afford the Splendid (especially in off-season). This 62-room, gleaming white hotel was renovated a few years ago, and has views overlooking the harbor. *Info: 4-6 rue Félix-Faure. www.splendid-*

hotel-cannes.fr. Tel. 04/97.06.22.22. V, MC, AE. AC, TV, telephone, Internet, in-room safe, hairdryer.

La Mère Besson €€-€€€
Old favorite serving Provençal dishes. Fantastic duck-breast dishes. *Info:13 rue des Frères-Pradignac (a few streets north of the waterfront).Tel. 04/93.39.59.24. Closed Sun. Reservations required.*

Au Bec Fin €€
Unpretentious bistro (in a town of lots of pretentious restaurants) serving traditional French cuisine. Info: 12 rue du 24-Août. Tel. 04/93.38.35.86. Closed Sun and mid-Dec to mid-Jan.

COGOLIN
Le Ferme du Magnan €€
Ten minutes from St-Tropez, this restaurant specializes in Provençal country cooking and is located on a hilltop farm. Definitely worth the drive. *Info: On route N98 in Cogolin (6 miles (9 km) west of St-Tropez). Tel. 04/94.49.57.54. Closed mid-Oct to Mar.*

FRÉJUS
Les Potiers €€
In a town filled with restaurants and cafés catering to beachgoers, this tiny, charming restaurant away from the beach serves French and Provençal dishes in a 15th-century stone house. *Info: 135 rue des Potiers (in the Old Town). Tel. 04/94.51.33.74. Closed Tue and Wed (lunch).*

GOURDON
Le Nid d'Aigle €€-€€€
Although the cannelloni and langoustines on the menu are delicious, it's the location on a terrace perched on the edge of a hill that makes this restaurant so special. The

SLEEPS & EATS

name means "Eagle's Nest." You'd be hard-pressed to find a more dramatic setting for a restaurant. *Info: place Victoria. Tel. 04/ 93.77.52.02. Closed Mon and Tue from mid-Sep to mid-June.*

GRASSE
La Bastide St-Antoine €€€

A 200-year-old farmhouse and inn (the Rolling Stones once

stayed here) is the site of an award-winning restaurant. There are nine luxury rooms and seven suites. *Info: 48 avenue Henri-Dunant. www.jacques-chibois.com. Tel.* 04/93.70.94.94. V, MC, DC, AE. *AC, TV, telephone, minibar, in-room safe, hairdryer, Internet.*

GRIMAUD
Le Côteau Fleuri €€-€€€

Attractive hotel/restaurant located on the quiet place des Pénitents serving Mediterranean fare. *Info: place des Pénitents. Tel. 04/ 94.43.20.17. Closed mid-Nov to mid-Dec and Tue (except in high season).*

La Bretonnière €€-€€€

Traditional Provençal fare at this lovely restaurant. Delicious lamb dishes. *Info: place des Pénitents. Tel. 04/94.43.25.26. Closed in off-season.*

HAUT-DE-CAGNES
Le Grimaldi €€

Indoor and outdoor dining on the Old Town square at this family-owned restaurant/inn serving local specialties. Try the lapin (*rabbit*). There are also many other cafés on the square. *Info: 6 place du Château in Haut-de-Cagnes. Tel. 04/93.20.60.24. Closed Nov, mid-Jan to mid-Feb.*

JUAN-LES-PINS
Le Perroquet €€
The name of the restaurant means "the parakeet" (if you couldn't tell that from its décor). Provençal dishes in a casual setting. The house specialty is grilled fish. *Info: avenue Georges-Gallice (across from Parc de la Pinède). Tel. 04/93.61.02.20. Closed mid-Nov to end of Dec.*

MOUGINS
Le Moulin de Mougins €€€
This inn has four suites and three rooms. Most are filled with those dining at the restaurant of the same name, as this is *the*

place to come for a luxurious dinner when staying in Cannes or Mougin. The inn, restaurant and cooking school is in a 16th-century olive mill surrounded by mimosas and palms. If it's good enough for Sharon Stone and Elizabeth Taylor, it should be good enough for you. Acclaimed chef Roger Verfé (who helped promote Provençal cuisine throughout the world) began this restaurant and now Chef Alain Llorca serves his innovative dishes here. *Info: Notre-Dame-de-Vie (1 mile southeast of Mougins and 4 miles inland from Cannes). www.moulin-mougins.com. Tel. 04/93.75.78.24. V, MC, DC, AE. TV, AC, minibar.*

ST-PAUL-DE-VENCE
Auberge Le Hameau €€
This former farmhouse on the outskirts of town provides an oh, so Riviera experience. Some of the 17 rooms and suites have terraces facing the lovely outdoor pool; others have views of St-Paul or the Mediterranean Sea. Rooms are decorated with Provençal furniture. *Info: 528 Route D107 (a little less than 1 mile from St-Paul in the direction of Colle). www.le-hameau.com.*

Tel. 04/93.32.80.24. V, MC. Bar, outdoor pool, AC, TV, gym, telephone, minibar, hairdryer, safe, wireless Internet. Closed mid-Nov to mid-Feb.

La Colombe d'Or €€€

This exclusive, family-run 26-room villa is just 12 miles from Nice, and is surrounded by cypress trees. Beautiful outdoor pool.

Cozy rooms decorated with ceramic tile. Most come here for its restaurant, with art of such notables as Picasso and Utrillo on the walls. *Info: 1 place du Général-de-Gaulle. www.la-colombe-dor.com. Tel. 04/ 93.32.80.02. V, MC, DC, AE. Restaurant, bar, outdoor pool, AC, TV, telephone, minibar, hairdryer, safe. Closed Nov and Dec.*

ST-TROPEZ

Le Byblos €€€

Trying to get into one of the 52 rooms or 43 suites at this hotel can be a challenge (almost as hard as getting into its' Caves du Roy nightclub). If you manage to get in, you'll share the place with celebrities and guests on expense accounts. Modern, comfortable and glamorous. There are two restaurants, including the highly acclaimed and expensive **Spoon Byblos** *(Tel. 04/ 94.56.68.20). Info: Ave. Paul-Signac. www.byblos.com. Tel. 04/ 94.56.68.00. V, MC, DC, AE. Restaurants, bar, outdoor pool, AC, cable TV, telephone, gym, minibar, hairdryer, safe, Internet access. Closed mid-Oct to Easter.*

Hôtel Le Yaca €€€

This former private home was built in 1722. It was once the meeting place of Impressionist painters such as Paul Signac. The 28-room hotel is situated on a small street in the Old Town. Many of the rooms have views of the beautiful inner flower garden. Upper-floor rooms have views of the Gulf of St-Tropez. In July

and August, there's a shuttle service to the beach (or you can just hang out at the beautiful swimming pool). *Info: 1 blvd. D'Aumale. www.hotel-le-yaca.fr. Tel. 04/94.55.81.00. V, MC, DC, AE. Restaurant, bar, outdoor pool, AC, TV, telephone, minibar, hairdryer, safe, Internet access. Closed mid-Oct to mid-Apr.*

Hôtel Sube €€

Located on the port near the tourist office, this hotel has a lovely lounge and comfortable rooms (you'll pay more for a port view). Great location for shopping. *Info: 15 quai Suffren. Tel. 04/94.97.30.04. www.hotel-sube.com. V, MC, AE. Bar, AC, TV, telephone.*

Leï Mouscardins €€€

Located at the end of the harbor with stunning views, this formal restaurant serves excellent French, Mediterranean and Provençal cuisine, including *bouillabaisse*. *Info: 1 rue Portalet. Tel. 04/94.97.29.00. Closed Tue in winter, mid-Nov to mid-Dec, and mid-Jan to mid-Feb.*

Le Girelier €€

Grilled fish is the specialty at this family-owned restaurant on the port. You'll recognize it by its blue-and-white awning and décor. *Info: quai Jean-Jaurès (on the harbor). Tel. 04/94.97.03.87. Closed mid-Nov to mid-Dec. Moderate.*

Le Club 55 €€

A simple beachside seafood restaurant? Ask one of the celebrities that have eaten here. There's also a great shop selling everything you need for the beach. *Info: 55 boulevard Patch. plage de Pampelonne. Tel. 04/94.55.55.55. Moderate.*

SLEEPS & EATS

TERRE BLANCHE
Four Seasons Resort €€€

Golfers will be in heaven at the two 18-hole courses designed by

Dave Thomas. The resort, just south of Tourrettes and Fayence (19 miles [30 km] from Cannes and 35 miles [56 km] from Nice), offers everything a golf lover or non-golf lover could ever want. *Info: www.fourseasons.com/ provence. Tel. 04/ 94.39.90.00. V, MC, DC, AE. Restaurant, bar, room service, outdoor pool, gym, AC, TV, telephone, CD/DVD player, minibar, hairdryer, safe, Internet access.*

TOURRETTES-SUR-LOUP
Le Petit Manoir €€

In the center of town, this small, no-frills restaurant serves traditional French cuisine, especially game dishes. *Info: 21 Grande Rue. Tel. 04/93.24.19.19. Closed Wed and Sun (dinner) and mid-Nov to mid-Dec. Moderate.*

VENCE
La Farigoule €€-€€€

Classic Provençal cuisine with indoor and outdoor dining. The Provençal dish *pissaladière* (a pizza-like tart with onions, black olives and purée of anchovies and sardines) is a specialty here. *Info: 15 rue Henri-Isnard (in the Old Town). Tel. 04/93.58.01.27. Closed Tue.*

BEST SHOPPING

St-Tropez
Jacqueline Thienot
Interesting antiques from throughout the French Riviera. *Info: 2 rue Georges-Clemenceau. Tel. 04/ 94.97.05.70. Closed Sun.*

Kiwi
Sexy beach wear. *Info: 34 rue Allard. Tel 04/94.97.42.26*

Le Club 55
This restaurant has a connected shop selling everything you need for the beach. *Info: 55 boulevard Patch. plage de Pampelonne. Tel. 04/94.55.55.55. Moderate.*

Pause-Douceur
Fantastic French chocolates. *Info: 11 rue Allard, Tel. 04/94.97.27.58.*

Galeries Tropéziennes
Unusual gifts and clothes to bring home. *Info: 56 rue Gambetta, Tel. 04/94.97.02.21.*

La Maison des Lices
Provençal furniture, linens and household goods. *Info: 18 boulevard Louis-Blanc, Tel. 04/94.97.11.34.*

Reminiscence
Funky jewelry. *place la Garonne. Info: Tel. 04/94.97.21.57.*

The place des Lices along boulevard Vasserot is home to a lively **market**. On Tuesday and Saturday mornings, stalls sell everything from produce to antiques.

Antibes
Balade en Provence
Regional products are sold at this small shop along the covered market. You should go downstairs where there's a good selection of regional wines and a tasting room. *Info: 25 cours Massena. Tel. 04/93.34.93.00.*

The heart of Antibes is the 19th-century canopy of the **Marché Provençal** (Provence Market). Everything from flowers to produce to crafts to beachwear can be found here.

Cannes
Cannolive
Provençal products, especially olive oils, at this long-standing shop at 16 rue Vénizelos.

Le Marché Forville, a covered market not too far from Festival Hall, features a flea market (Mon) and a produce and flower market (Tue through Sun).

Biot
There are many shops selling pottery, ceramics and decorative glassware, and most of them are near the place des Arcades. You can watch glassblowers and purchase expensive glassware at **Verreries de Biot** at 5 chemin des Combes on the edge of town.

BEST NIGHTLIFE & ENTERTAINMENT

St-Tropez
Octave Café
Posh piano bar. *Info: Place de la Garonne. Tel. 04/ 94.97.22.56.*

Les Caves du Roy
If you can get in, you can drink and dance the night away at this bar/club in the Byblos Hotel. *Info: Ave. Paul-Signac. Tel. 04/94.56.68.00.*

Les Caves du Roy
If you can get in, you can dance the night away at this dance club in the Byblos Hotel. *Info: Ave. Paul-Signac. Tel. 04/94.56.68.00.*

L'Esquinade
Gay bar. *Info: 2 rue du Four, Tel. 04/94.97.87.45*

Cannes
Carlton
The grand hotel bar at the InterContinental Carlton Hotel. Glamorous and expen-sive. *Info: 58 La Croisette. Tel. 04/93.06.40.06.*

Le Bâoli
Get out your wallet and enjoy cocktails at this restaurant/ lounge and dance bar. *Info: Port Pierre Canto. www.lebaoli.com. Tel. 04/ 93.39.43.03.43.*

Le Hype
Gay bar. *Info: 52 blvd. Jean-Jaurès. Tel. 04/93.39.20.50.*

Le Sept
Gay bar and disco. *Info: 7 rue Rougière. Tel.04/93.39.10.36.*

Casino Action
• **Casino Croisette** and **Palm Beach Casino** in Cannes
• **Eden Casino** in Juan-les-Pins

BEST SPORTS & RECREATION

Cannes
Golf Club de
Cannes-Mandelieu
Golfers can enjoy two stunning golf courses (18 holes and 9 holes). *Info: 5 miles (8 km) northeast of Cannes on route D35. www.golfoldcourse.com. Tel. 04/92.97.32.00. Open daily.*

Antibes
Marineland
Whales, sharks, dolphins, sea lions, waterslides, miniature golf, petting zoo...you get the picture. Children will love it. *Info: On route N7 two miles (4 km) east of town. Tel. 04/93.33.49.49. Closed Oct-Jan but otherwise open daily. Admission: €36 adults, €28 children.*

SPORTS & RECREATION

10. NICE

HIGHLIGHTS

▲ Strolling on the Promenade des Anglais

▲ Wandering Nice's Old Town (Vieux Nice)

▲ Chagall paintings at the Musée National Message Biblique

▲ Avant-garde art at the Musée d'Art Moderne et d'Art Contemporain

▲ People-watching and dining on the colorful cours Saleya

INTRO

Why some avoid **Nice** is perplexing. It's 20 miles (33 km) northeast of Cannes/ 567 miles (912 km) south of Paris.

Nice, on the **Baie des Anges** (Bay of Angels), has on

COORDINATES

Nice (population 350,000) is in the south of France on the Mediterranean Sea, just 25 miles (40km) from the Italian border. It's 20 miles (33km) northeast of Cannes and 567 miles (912km) south of Paris.

average 300 sunny days a year, many important historical sights and museums, a fabulous Old Town, and great dining. Nice was part of Italy until 1860 and you'll see the Italian influence in everything from architecture to cuisine. Yes, it's a large city, but if you simply take time to experience it, you'll learn to love Nice.

A DAY IN NICE

*Begin your day at the **Jardin Albert-1er** on **the promenade des Anglais** between avenue de Verdun and boulevard Jean-Jaurès.*

Take in the sunbathers, runners and other walkers on the **promenade des Anglais**, the waterfront boulevard. Along the promenade is the **Jardin Albert 1er** (Albert I Garden). It's filled with exotic palms and flowers. Here, the promenade becomes the **quai des Etats-Unis**.

As you're heading toward the giant rock, turn left onto avenue des Phocéens and take the first right onto rue St-François-de-Paule.

You're now in Nice's **Old Town** (Vieux Nice). At number 14 (on your right) is **Alziari**, the place for fragrant olive oil (for sale in many sizes of blue and yellow tins), olive soap and olive spread. On your left at number 9 is

SIGHTS

SIGHTS

the beautiful **Eglise St-François-de-Paule** (also called Eglise des Dominicains), the sight of frequent classical concerts. Step inside and admire its beautiful interior. At number 7 (on your left) is the picturesque storefront of **Confiserie Auer**. This candy shop has been in business since 1820 and counts Queen Victoria as one of its famous customers.

At number 4 (on the right) is the oppulent **Opéra de Nice**. The four statues on top represent singing, music, dance and theatre, and the opera house is home to Nice's

chorus, orchestra, opera and ballet. Charles Garnier, the designer of this building, also created the famous opera house in Paris and the casino in Monte Carlo.

Continue down rue St-François-de-Paule to the cours Saleya.

To your left is the **Palais des Ducs de Savoie** (Dukes of Savoy Palace), parts of which date back to 1559.

The colorful **cours Saleya** is the main street of Old Nice and has been since the Middle Ages. It's home to a wonderful

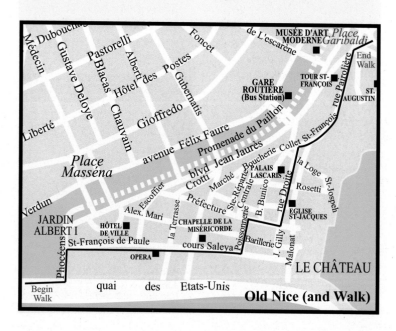

Old Nice (and Walk)

daily flower and food market. On Mondays, it's an antiques market. Stop at one of the many cafés that line the street.

On your left on the cours Saleya is the **Chapelle de la Miséricorde.** Stop in and take in the chapel's splendor. It's filled with chandeliers, faux marble, frescoes and carved woods, and it's one of the world's best examples of the Baroque style. *Info: cours Saleya. Open daily. Admission: Free.*

See that yellow stone building at the end of cours Saleya? Artist **Henri Matisse** lived there from 1921 to 1938. Before leaving the cours Saleya, sample *socca*, a crêpe

made with chickpea flour. Although there are several places that serve *socca*, you'll want to try one made by **Thérèse**, the legendary socca merchant of Old Nice. Her stand is often set up in front of La Cambuse restaurant (on the left side of the cours Saleya).

Turn left at rue de la Poissonnière.

On this small street is **Eglise Notre-Dame de l'Annonciation** (on your left). Check out the church's elaborate interior. *Info: 1 rue de la Poissonerie. Open daily. Admission: Free.*

Turn right onto rue de la Préfecture and then left onto rue Droite.

At the intersection of rue Droite and place du Jésus is **Eglise du Jésus** (Gesu). Stop in if you haven't had enough churches. *Info: Open daily. Admission: Free.*

At 15 rue Droite (on your left) is the sumptuous **Palais Lascaris**, built in the 17th century. The palace is filled with tapestries and statues, and has one of the grandest staircases you'll ever see. *Info: 15 rue Droite. Tel. 04/*

SIGHTS

Train Touristique

If you don't want to walk to the sights of Nice, try the rubber-wheeled tourist train (Train Touristique de Nice). It departs at least once every hour (except from Nov through Jan) from the Jardin Albert-1er (Albert I Garden) near the waterfront. The trip takes 40 minutes and passes many of Nice's main sights and costs €7.

93.62.72.40. Closed Tue. Admission: Free.

Continue on rue Droite until it ends and turn right onto rue St-François which turns into rue Pairolière.

You'll pass the **Tour St-François** (Tower of St. Francis) on your left at the square Jardin Auguste Icarte.

Continue down rue Pairolière.

The large square that you enter is **Place Garibaldi** (at rue Cassini). This very Italian-looking square was created at the end of the 18th century. In the center stands a statue and fountain of Joseph Garibaldi, an Italian patriot. You can take a break here at one of the cafés.

In the afternoon, visit one, or both, of these museums by famous artists with connections to this city. Both museums are in the Cimiez area of Nice.

The **Musée Matisse,** located in a 17th-century villa (*photo below*), contains the largest collection of paintings by Henri Matisse, who spent the last years of his life in Nice, and some of his personal effects are on display. Everything from his works as a student to his late-life works – from nudes to religious art – is featured here. *Info: 164 avenue des Arènes-de-Cimiez (in Cimiez). www.musee-matisee-nice.org. Tel. 04 93.53.40.53.*

Open Wed-Mon 10am-6pm. Closed Tue. Admission: Free.

Russian painter Marc Chagall (who later became a French citizen) donated the collection at **Musée National Message Biblique–Marc Chagall** to France, and it's among the largest anywhere. He was often influenced by Jewish themes, and you'll find his "Biblical Message" on display here. The museum has lovely gardens filled with herbs, olive trees and pools. *Info: avenue du Dr-Ménard (in Cimiez). www.musee-chagall.fr. Tel. 04/93.53.87.20. Open Wed-Mon May-Oct 10am-6pm (Nov-Apr until 5pm. Closed Tue. Admission: €7.*

If you want to shop, try one of these boutique-lined streets: rue Paradis, rue de Verdun, rue Masséna, and avenue Jean-Médecin.

For dinner, head back to the restaurants lining the cours Saleya in Old Nice.

A WEEKEND IN NICE

Friday Evening

Old Nice is home to many fine restaurants. After dinner, wander the streets of Old Nice. There are plenty of cafés where you can have a nightcap.

Saturday

Begin your morning at the **Promenade des Anglais**. This wide boulevard runs four miles along the entire length of **Nice's waterfront**. The name means "walkway of the English" because it was financed by wealthy English tourists who came here in droves in the 1800s in search of sun and sea. Today it's a beautiful walk made all the more interesting by sunbathers, walkers, runners and skaters from so many different parts of the world.

Oh, and put your eyes back into your head. While nudity is prohibited, topless bathing is not. The beaches here are made up of large uncomfortable rocks. Along the promenade is

SIGHTS

the **Jardin Albert-1er** (Albert I Garden). It's filled with exotic palms and flowers. At the east end of the promenade it becomes the **quai des Etats-Unis**.

Then head into **Vieux Nice** (Old Nice) to visit the colorful **cours Saleya**, the main street here since the Middle Ages. You must come here if you visit Nice. At times it seems that everyone in Nice is here, especially at night when its restaurants and cafés fill with locals and tourists. It's the home to a wonderful daily flower and food market. On Mondays, it's an antique market. Walk through the maze of narrow streets in Old Nice past small churches and under drying laundry for photo opportunities at every turn.

Have lunch at one of the many restaurants on the cours Saleya.

If you're not interested in lunch, try some of the best ice cream in the world. Family-owned **Glacier Fenocchio** has two locations in Old Nice. The main shop is at 2 place Rossetti facing the Cathédrale de Ste-Réparate. A second shop is just off the cours Saleya at 6 rue de la Poissonerie. Be adventurous and try one of the unique flavors like lavender, tomato, jasmin, or

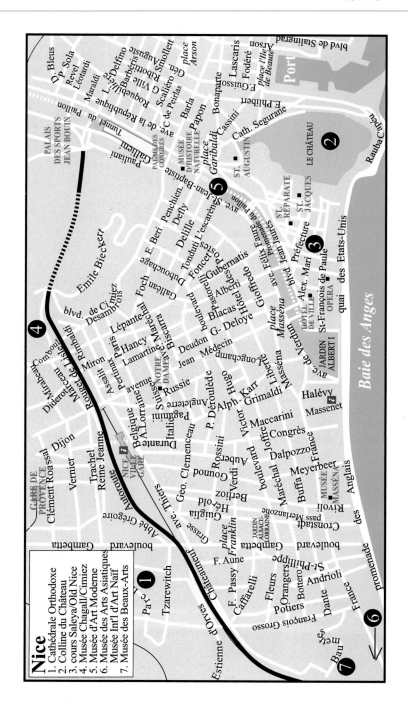

Nice
1. Cathédrale Orthodoxe
2. Colline du Château
3. cours Saleya/Old Nice
4. Musée Chagall/Cimiez
5. Musée d'Art Moderne
6. Musée des Arts Asiatiques
7. Musée Int'l d'Art Naïf
8. Musée des Beaux-Arts

comté de nice (studded with pine nuts and candied mandarin). *Info: Tel. 04/ 93.80.72.52.*

In the afternoon head to **Cimiez**, a hilltop neighborhood located in the northeast part of town. The easiest way to get here (it's about three miles north of Old Nice) is to take bus numbers 15 or 17 from place Masséna. You'll find the **Parc des Antiquités** at the top of the hill. This former arena and its gardens contain Roman ruins dating back to the first century.

Cimiez is home to two museums by famous artists with connections to this city.

If you're interested in the art of Marc Chagall, you can visit the **Musée National Message Biblique–Marc Chagall**. Russian painter Marc Chagall (who later became a French citizen) donated this collection to France, and it's among the largest anywhere. He was often influenced by Jewish themes, and you'll find his "Biblical Message" on display here. The museum has lovely gardens filled with herbs, olive trees and pools. *Info: avenue du Dr-Ménard (in Cimiez). www.musee-chagall.fr. Tel. 04/ 93.53.87.20. Open Wed-Mon May-Oct 10am-6pm (Nov-Apr until 5pm. Closed Tue. Admission: €7.*

The largest collection of paintings by Henri Matisse is at the **Musée Matisse**, located in a 17th-century villa. Matisse spent the last years of his life in Nice, and some of his personal effects are on display. Everything from his works as a student to his late-life works – from nudes to religious art – is featured here. *Info: 164 avenue des Arènes-de-Cimiez (in Cimiez). www.musee-matisee-nice.org. Tel. 04 93.53.40.53. Open Wed-Mon 10am-6pm. Closed Tue. Admission: Free.*

Another sight in Cimiez also has a Matisse connection: The **Musée Franciscain/Église et Monastère de Cimiez**. This Franciscan monastery is still home to monks. There are lovely gardens with panoramic views (Matisse is buried in the cemetery), a museum dedicated to the history of the Franciscan order, and a 15th-century church with elegant works by Bréa. *Info: place du Monastère (in Cimiez). Tel. 04/ 93.81.00.04. Church: Open daily 9am-6pm. Museum open Mon-Sat 10am-noon and 3pm-6pm. Closed Sun. Admission: Free.*

If you're more interested in archeology, you can head to the **Musée Archéologique.** It's filled with Roman finds from the Cimiez area. *Info: 160 avenue des Arènes-de-Cimiez (in Cimiez). Tel. 04/ 93.81.59.57. Open Wed-Mon 10am-6pm. Closed Tue. Admission: Free.*

If you don't want to make the trek to Cimiez, you can visit the **Musée des Arts Asiatiques**, where you'll find Asian paintings, sculpture, carvings and ceramics. The museum is housed in a sleek modern building built on an artificial lake in the 17-acre Parc Phoenix, a botanical garden. *Info: 405 promenade des Anglais. Tel. 04/ 92.29.37.00. Open May to mid-Oct Wed-Mon 10am-6pm (mid-Oct to Apr until*

5pm). Closed Tue. Admission: Free.

For those interested in elegant dining, make reservations at **Le Chantecler**, Nice's most prestigious restaurant located in the luxurious **Hôtel Negresco** (try **Le Relais** here for a cocktail). Even if you don't dine or drink here, step inside and admire this incredible hotel. From the lobby, you can visit the Salon Royal with its immense 19th-century Baccarat crystal chandelier and dome. *Info: 37 promenade des Anglais.*

You can gamble the night away at the modern **Casino Ruhl**. *Info: On the waterfront at 1 promenade des Anglais. Tel. 04/97.03.12.22.*

Sunday
If you're not going to spend some time on the beach in Nice (and, yes, they are topless), then Sunday is a great day to see some of the city's other museums.

On the west side of town is the **Musée des Beaux-Arts Jules-Chéret** (Jules-Chéret Fine Arts Museum). Housed in a 19th-century mansion, it contains works of former

SIGHTS

residents of the city (including those of the man from whom the museum takes its name). Artists on display include Monet, Degas and Renoir. There are also ceramic works by Picasso, and sculpture by Rodin. *Info: 33 avenue des Baumettes. Tel. 04/92.15.28.28. Open Tue-Sun 10am-6pm. Closed Mon. Admission: €5.*

If contemporary art is more to your liking, visit the **Musée d'Art Moderne et d'Art Contemporain**. You can't miss the contemporary structures (four gray marble towers) that house this museum of avant-garde art from the 1960s to today. *Info: promenade des Arts. Tel. 04/97.13.42.01. Open Tue-Sun 10am-6pm. Closed Mon. Admission: Free.*

High on a rock above the city are the ruins of a castle that was destroyed in 1706. The ruins are now a park and gardens called **Colline du Château**. You have fantastic views of the foothills of the Alps, the bay, the waterfront promenade and the red-tile roofs of Old Nice. You can take an elevator to the top of this hill for €1. The elevator is on the quai des Etats-Unis just

to the left of the Hôtel Suisse. *Info: Colline du Château. Open daily. Admission: Free.*

The **Musée de la Marine** (Naval Museum) is located in the **Tour Bellanda** (Bellanda Tower) halfway up to Colline du Château. It has a collection of model boats, paintings and weapons all related to the navy. French composer Hector Berlioz lived in this tower for a year in 1844. *Info: Tel. 04/93.80.47.61. Closed Mon and Tue. Admission: €3.*

Further afar and of special interest to some are these two sights outside the city center.

You'll know when you're getting close to the **Cathédrale Orthodoxe Russe St-Nicolas** (Russian Orthodox Cathedral), as you can't help but notice its onion-shaped domes, so out of place on the Riviera. In 1912, Czar Nicholas II gave the cathedral to the large Russian community who lived and vacationed here. You'll feel like you're in Russia (or at least not in Nice) when you step into its interior, filled with icons and incense. *Info: avenue Nicolas-II at 17 boulevard du Tzaréwitch. Tel.*

04/93.96.88.02. Open daily (closed to tourists Sun mornings). Admission: €3.

The **Musée International d'Art Naïf Anatole-Jakovsky** is named after an art critic, and houses his collection of over 600 works of naïve art. You'll find everything from primitive paintings to American folk art here. *Info: avenue de Fabron (in the Château St-Héléne). Tel. 04/93.71.78.33. Open Wed-Mon 10am-6pm. Closed Tue. Admission: €4.*

For dinner, the cours Saleya is just the place to end your weekend in Nice.

BEST SLEEPS & EATS

NICE
La Palais de la Mediterranée €€€
This Art Deco casino was turned into a hotel in 2004. Fantastic views of the sea from its prime location on the Promenade des Anglais (Nice's seafront street and walkway), near Old Nice. Great outdoor pool.

Its restaurant, **Le Padouk**, serves Mediterranean and Asian cuisine on the poolside terrace. *Info: 13-15 Promenade des Anglais. www.lepalaisdelamediterranee.com. Tel. 04/92.14.77.00. V, MC, AE. Restaurant, bar, outdoor pool, AC, TV, telephone, minibar, in-room safe, hairdryer, wireless Internet.*

La Perouse €€€
This charming hotel is tucked into the hillside below the *château*, just a short walk from Old Nice. Great location, helpful staff, and a lovely pool. *Info: 11 quai Rauba-Capeau. www.hotel-la-perouse.com. Tel. 04/93.62.34.63. V, MC, DC, AE. Restaurant, bar, outdoor pool, TV, telephone, minibar, hairdryer, safe, wireless Internet.*

SLEEPS & EATS

Hôtel Negresco €€€

The grand dame of Nice hotels. Located on the promenade des

Anglais, this luxurious hotel will pamper you in style. It's home to the Salon Royal with its immense 19th-century Baccarat crystal chandelier and dome. **Le Chantecler**, Nice's most prestigious restaurant, is also located here, along with the elegant **Le Relais**. *Info: 37 promenade des Anglais. www.hotel-negresco-nice.com. Tel. 04/93.16.64.00. V, MC, DC, AE. Restaurants, bar, gym, AC, TV, telephone, minibar, hairdryer, Internet.*

Hôtel Gounod €€

Built in the early 1900s, this 45-room hotel is a good, moderately priced choice in Nice's central city. It's about a five-minute walk to the beach. Comfortable and quiet guest rooms, and an added bonus is that guests can use the pool at the Hôtel Splendid next door. *Info: 3 rue Gounod. www.gounod-nice.com. Tel. 04/93.16.42.00. V, MC, DC, AE. Restaurant, bar, gym, AC, TV, telephone, minibar, hairdryer. Closed mid-Nov to mid-Dec.*

Hôtel de la Buffa €

This hotel, popular with families, has 13 no-nonsense rooms with private baths with showers. It's located just off the promenade des Anglais and the beach. Public parking lot is nearby. *Info: 56 rue de la Buffa (off of blvd. Gambetta). www.hotel-buffa.com. Tel. 04/93.88.77.35. V, AE. AC, TV, telephone, hairdryer, Internet access.*

Villa Saint-Exupéry €

Budget travelers can stay at this student residence and former monastery in the summer, when it opens its doors to visitors. Both

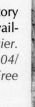

basic rooms and dormitory communal rooms are available. *Info: 22 ave. Gravier. www.vsaint.com. Tel. 04/ 93.84.42.83. V, MC. Free Internet access.*

Le Balcon Grand €€€
You'll find innovative cuisine in a romantic setting at this restaurant. Try the duck in pear sauce or the chicken with chanterelle mushrooms in a cream sauce. *Info: 10 rue St-François-de-Paule. Tel. 04/93.62.60.74. Closed Sat (lunch) and Sun (lunch).*

Le Chantecler €€€
Nice's most prestigious restaurant located in the luxurious Hôtel Negresco. *Info: 37 promenade des Anglais. Tel. 04/93.16.64.00. Closed Mon, Tue and Jan to mid-Feb. Reservations required.*

La Cambuse €€-€€€
Located on the busy cours Saleya, this restaurant serves Niçoise and traditional French dishes. *Info: 5 cours Saleya. Tel. 04/ 93.80.82.40. Open daily.*

La Merenda €€-€€€
This tiny bistro, run by the former chef at the Hôtel Negresco, has no phone. You have to stop by to make reservations in person, but it's worth it. Innovative cuisine, fresh ingredients and attentive service. *Info: 4 rue Raoul Bosio (formeryl rue de la Terrasse. No phone. No credit cards. Closed weekends, parts of Feb and Aug and two weeks at Christmas and New Year's.*

Le Tire Bouchon €€-€€€
This tiny bistro serves the specialties of southwest France. The *cassoulet* (a meat, bean and sausage casserole) is fantastic. *Info: 19 rue de la*

Préfecture. www.le-tire-bouchon.com. Tel. 04/93.92.63.64. Open daily. No lunch.

La Perouse €€-€€€

This charming hotel restaurant is tucked into the hillside below the *château*, just a short walk from Old Nice. You can dine on its

terrace under lemon trees. *Info: 11 quai Rauba-Capeau. www.hotel-la-perouse.com. Tel. 04/93.62.34.63. Dinner only. Closed Nov-Mar.*

La Petite Maison €€

Once a grocery store, this popular bistro/tavern serves authentic local dishes. Try the *fleurs de courgette farcies*, zucchini flowers stuffed with cheese. Delicious! *Info: 11 rue St-François-de-Paule. www.lapetitemaison-nice.com. Tel. 04/93.92.59.59 Closed Sun.*

Don Camillo €€

Located off the cours Saleya in Old Nice, it specializes in local dishes. Try the cheese platter. *Info: 5 rue des Ponchettes. www.doncamillo-creations.fr. Tel. 04/93.85.67.95. Closed Sun and Mon.*

Le Safari €€

Dine on Provençal and Niçoise specialties at this popular restaurant overlooking the flower market. I have eaten here frequently and never had a bad meal. The people-watching is great. *Info: 1 cours Saleya. Tel. 04/93.80.18.44. Open daily.*

Pasta Basta €

Good, hearty pasta dishes and pizza (and not a bad house wine either). *Info: 18 rue de la Préfecture. Tel. 04/93.80.03.57. Open daily.*

BEST SHOPPING

There are many antique shops on **rue Catherine Ségurane** and **rue Emmanuel Philibert**.

Galeries Lafayette
This upscale department store has a wonderful food court in the basement and a restaurant on the fourth floor. *Info: 6 avenue Jean Médelin. Closed Sun.*

Confiserie Henri-Auer
This fantastic candy and chocolate shop near the opera house has been in business since 1820. *Info: 7 rue St-François-de-Paule. Tel. 04/93.85.77.98. Closed Sun.*

The colorful **cours Saleya** (the main street of Old Nice) has a wonderful daily **flower and food market**. On Mondays, it's an antiques market.

BEST NIGHTLIFE & ENTERTAINMENT

Le Relais
If you're looking for an elegant place to have a cocktail, try the bar at the Hôtel Negresco. *Info: 37 promenade des Anglais. Tel. 04/93.16.64.00.*

Le Before
Trendy aperitif bar. *Info: 18 rue des Congrès. Tel. 04/93.87.85.59.*

Le Master Home Bar
Noisy sports bar with occasional live performances. *Info: 11 rue de la Prefecture. Tel. 04/93.80.33.82.*

Casino Ruhl
You can gamble the night away at the modern Casino Ruhl on the waterfront, at 1 promenade des Anglais. *Info: Tel. 04/97.03.12.22.*

SHOPPING

NIGHTLIFE & ENTERTAINMENT

NIGHTLIFE & ENTERTAINMENT

Events in Nice

- **Carnaval**, Nice's Mardi Gras, takes place the weeks leading up to Ash Wednesday
- **Nice Jazz Festival**, held for a week in mid-July. *Info: www.nicejazzfestival.fr*
- Nice's **Opera** (Opéra de Nice) performs from September to June at the opera house (*photo below*). *Info: 4 rue St-François-de-Paule. Tel. 04/92.17.40.00*

Disco Butterfly
Long-standing popular dance club. Gets going quite late, like most clubs here. *Info: 67 que de Etats-Unis. Tel. 04/93.92.27.34.*

Les Trois Diables
On the cours Saleya, the main street of Old Nice. A bar, restaurant and dance club. *Info: 2 cours Saleya. Tel. 04/93.62.47.00.*

L'Ambassade
More sophisticated than most clubs here, so dress appropriately. *Info: 18 rue du Congrès. Tel. 04/93.88.88.87.*

Opéra de Nice
This opulent opera house was designed by Charles Garnier, who also designed the famous opera house in Paris and the casino in Monte Carlo. The four statues on top represent singing, music, dance and theatre, and the opera house is home to Nice's chorus, orchestra, opera and ballet. *Info: 4 rue St-François-de-Paule. Tel. 04/92.17.40.00. Open for performances.*

There are a number of popular gay establishments in Nice: **Keep in Touch**, *5 rue Halevy. Tel. 04/93.87.07.04* (bar); **Le Klub**, *6 rue Halevy. Tel.04/60.55.26.61* (bar and disco); **Le Blue Boy**, *9 rue Jean-Baptiste Spinetta. Tel.04/93.44.68.24* (bar and disco); **Le Block**, *10 rue Gilly (at cours Saleya). Tel. 04/93.80.18.55* (cruisy bar); **Sapho**, *2 rue Colonna d'Istra. Tel. 04/93.62.58.42* (women). For more information on gay bars, clubs, and rental apartments in Nice, see the *Nice Gay Guide* section of www.absoluliving.com.

11. THE EASTERN FRENCH RIVIERA

HIGHLIGHTS

▲ Slow down in St-Jean-Cap-Ferrat

▲ An ideal town on the sea: Villefranche-sur-Mer

▲ Magnificent Eze, peaceful La Turbie, and sedate Menton

▲ Glitzy Monaco

INTRO

The French lifestyle with an Italian feel greets you in this part of the French Riviera. We'll visit villages east of Nice up to the border and reaching down to the sea. Some of the highlights here include the lovely hillop **Eze**,

upscale **St-Jean-Cap-Ferrat**, and the quaint harbor town of **Villefranche-sur-Mer**. Then we'll cross the border to visit swanky **Monaco**, and have lunch in **Italy**.

The eastern half of the **Côte d'Azur** offers great beaches, beautiful hilltop villages and renowned gardens. Visit the unique principality of **Monaco**, or shoot over the border and visit **Ventimiglia** in Italy to eat lunch or shop!

A WEEK ON THE EASTERN FRENCH RIVIERA

St-Jean-Cap-Ferrat

We're going to slow down in **St-Jean-Cap-Ferrat**, 1 mile (2 km) south of Beaulieu/6 miles (10 km) east of Nice.

The residents of this port village on the peninsula Cap-Ferrat live here for its warm climate and beautiful sea views. Its promenades are lined with cafés and restaurants, and its port is filled with pleasure craft. It's home to luxurious hotels including the **Grand Hôtel du Cap-Ferrat**, located at the tip of the peninsula. Most of the villas are hidden by gates and lush vegetation. Unlike nearby towns, the pace here is not at all hectic. The beaches here are pebbly, not sandy, and there's a coastal walkway if you want to walk around the cape.

While here, visit the **Villa Ephrussi de Rothschild/Musée Ile-de-France**, a palace by the sea (*photo below*). This Italian-style villa was left to the French

SIGHTS

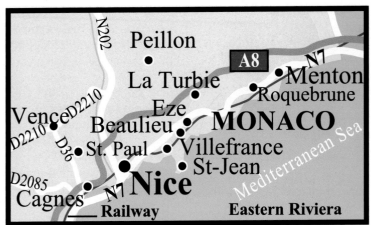

Eastern Riviera

government by Baroness Rothschild, and includes over 5,000 works of art. Fabulous gardens with ornamental lakes and waterfalls surround the villa. *Info: avenue Denis-Séméria. www.villa-ephrussi.com. Tel. 04/93.01.33.09. Open daily mid-Feb to Oct 10am-6pm (Jul and Aug until 7pm). Nov-mid to Feb Mon-Fri 2pm-6pm, Sat and Sun 10am-6pm. Admission: €10. Combined admission with Villa Kérylos is €15.*

Villefranche-sur-Mer
We'll visit two towns on the sea ("sur mer"). First, let's head to **Villefranche-sur-Mer**, a wonderful harbor town, 6 miles (10 km) east of Nice.

The city looks Italian with its yellow and ochre homes reaching down the hill to the

sea. The beach here is pebbly, and the harbor can accommodate huge vessels. It's still a naval port. The interesting **rue Obscure**, a street that runs parallel to the waterfront, is covered by vaulted arcades (it's

SIGHTS

Driving Around

The **coastline east of Nice** is a huge cliff with three parallel highways (note: if you want to travel at high speeds from the Italian border all the way past Cannes, making day trips easy, take Route A8):

Grande Corniche – the highest and fastest, with the fewest places to enjoy the view.

Moyenne Corniche – the middle road offering shore views and passing through several towns, including the beautiful and popular Èze.

Basse Corniche – the lowest where you crawl (especially in July and August) through one picturesque resort after another.

just off rue de l'Eglise). The town has a huge restored citadel (**Citadelle St- Elme**) dating from the 16th-century, housing municipal offices and five free museums dedicated

to local history. There's also a lively market on Sundays at place Amélie Pollonais.

Jean Cocteau decorated the walls of **Chapelle St-Pierre**, a Romanesque church, in the 1950s with images of St. Peter. *Info: quai de la Douane/place Pollonais/rue des Marinières. Tel. 04/93.76.90.70. Closed Mon and mid-Nov to mid-Dec. Admission: €2.*

Take a break at **La Mère Germaine** on the waterfront or at the wine bar on the port at the **Hôtel Welcome**.

Beaulieu-sur-Mer

After visiting Villefranche, head to nearby **Beaulieu-sur-Mer**, just two miles (four km) east of Villefrance-sur-Mer.

This village is referred to as "La Petite Afrique" (Little Africa) owing to its warm climate and lush vegetation. The Alpes-Maritimes mountains descend-

ing to the coast shelter this resort town. The stroll along the seafront promenade lets you glimpse lovely villas, most of which are hidden by vegetation and fences. The Art Deco **Casino de Beaulieu** was built in 1903 (no beach attire). The town has two churches, the 12th-century chapel **Santa Maria de Olivo**, and the 19th-century **Eglise du Sacré-Coeur**.

In a town with incredible villas, the **Villa Kérylos** stands out. Step inside for a look. It's an imitation of a Greek villa from Classical times, and contains some Greek antiquities brought here in 1900 when the villa was built by an archeologist. Definitely unusual! *Info: rue Gustave-Eiffel (at the tip of the bay). www.villa-kerylos.com. Tel. 04/93.01.01.44. Open daily mid-Feb to Oct 10am-6pm (Jul and Aug until 7pm). Nov to mid-Feb Mon-Fri 2pm-6pm, Sat and Sun 10am-6pm). Admission: €9 (with audio guide). Combined admission with Villa Ephrussi is €15.*

Eze

Today you'll visit the most magnificent hilltop village, **Eze**. It's 4 miles (7 km) west of Monte Carlo/7 miles (11 km) east of Nice (via the Moyenne Corniche).

To say that Eze has a magnificent hilltop location is an understatement. This tiny fortified village towers over the surrounding countryside with unbelievable views of the sea. It's the highest of the area's perched villages. You'll enter through the town gate (designed to keep the Turks out). Most of this rocky village dates back to the 14th century. On your way to the top is the tiny **Chapelle de la Ste-Croix**,

SIGHTS

SIGHTS

the former seat of a lay brotherhood that wore white habits and performed good deeds The church of **Notre-Dame de l'Assomption** (built in 1764) has a Baroque interior. A web of narrow streets passes stone houses converted to boutiques, galleries and souvenir shops. It's touristy and, in high season, the narrow streets can get quite cramped, but the view from the hilltop castle ruins are worth it.

For the adventurous, there's a walk on an old mule trail from Eze to **Eze-Bord-de-Mer** on the coast. Look for signs for **Sentier Fédéric Nietzsche**. You begin at the entry to town (just to the left of the entrance to the luxury hotel Château de la Chèvre d'Or). The walk takes at least an hour each way and although beautiful, is only for the fit. If you're not up to the entire walk, just head down a bit for a great view of the coast.

Make sure to visit the **Jardin Exotique** at the hilltop castle ruins (*photo above*). This densely planted flower and cactus garden (with English descriptions), along with whimsical statuary, affords spectacular views. Don't miss it! *Info: Tel. 04/93.41.10.30. Open daily 9am-sunset. Admission: €5.*

There are some good choices for dining in Eze. **Loumiri** is near the entry to the old village, or you can try **Hostellerie du Château de la Chèvre d'Or** on rue du Barri, an incredible luxury-hotel complex of stone houses with several restaurants, including the renowned and expensive Restaurant de la Chèvre d'Or. If you don't eat here, have a drink at sunset at the outdoor cliffside hotel bar – but there's a steep minimum drink order on weekends.

Monaco

Today we'll spend the day in **Monaco**, the capital of glitz. It's 12 miles (19 km) east of Nice.

Monaco mixes aristocratic glitz and a little bit of Las Vegas. It's the second-smallest state in Europe; only Vatican City is smaller. This principality is bordered by France and the Mediterranean Sea, takes up less than one square mile, and is nestled against mountains that seem to push it into the sea. High-rises attest to the fact that there's nowhere to go but up in this tiny country. Residents (Monégasques), of which there are less than 10,000, pay no taxes.

There are four parts of the principality: **Monte Carlo**, home to the famous casino and ultra-luxury hotels; **Fontvieille**, an industrial suburb; **Monaco-Ville**, the location of government buildings and the royal palace; and **La Condamine**, at the port where most Monégasques live. Monaco's location is fantastic, its weather incredible (on average, 310 sunny days a year) and crime is virtually unheard of (there's one policeman for every 100 residents).

Bus service is available within Monaco for €1 (10 tickets for €6), with stops at every tourist sight. To figure out which one to take, simply look at the name on the front of the bus.

Head to the **Place du Palais**. This square offers views of the palace and contains a **statue of Francesco Grimaldi**. Francesco (they refer to him as François here) was an Italian who was kicked out of Genoa.

SIGHTS

SIGHTS

Grace Kelly

American film star **Grace Kelly** met **Prince Rainier** of Monaco while attending the Cannes International Film Festival to promote the Alfred Hitchcock film *To Catch a Thief*, which she starred in with Cary Grant. The film featured her racing along the Corniches. Soon after, in 1956, she married Prince Rainier, moved to Monaco, and had three children with him. Princess Grace was wildly popular among the Monégasques. Ironically, in 1982 she was killed while driving on the same Corniches featured in her film. The flower-decked tomb of Princess Grace is located at **Cathédrale de l'Immaculée-Conception**, a Romanesque-style church, which was also the site of her fairy-tale wedding to Prince Rainier in 1956. Prince Rainier was buried at her side in 2005. *Info: avenue St-Martin. Open daily. Admission: Free.*

He and his cohorts dressed up as monks in 1297 and seized the castle. This was the beginning of the Grimaldi dynasty, which continues to this day.

You can't miss **Le Rocher** (The Rock), crowned by the Prince's Palace. A medieval castle once stood where the **Palais Princier** is located. In the summer you can take a guided tour through the royal family's extravagant home. Included in the tour is a glimpse of the immense art collection, the throne room, the **royal apartments** (Les Grands Appartements) and the beautiful state portrait of Princess Grace. You can watch the colorful changing of the guard at around 11:45am to noon. Also in the palace is the **Napoleon Museum** (Musée Napoléonien), housing a collection of swords, medals, hats and other items which belonged to Napoleon. Monaco was occupied by Napoleon after the French Revolution. *Info: place du Palais. Tel. 377/93.25.18.31. Royal apartments: Open Apr 11:30am-6pm, May-Sep 9:30am-6:30pm, Oct 10am-5:30pm. Closed Nov-Mar. Admission: €7. Museum: Open daily Jun-Sep 9:30am-*

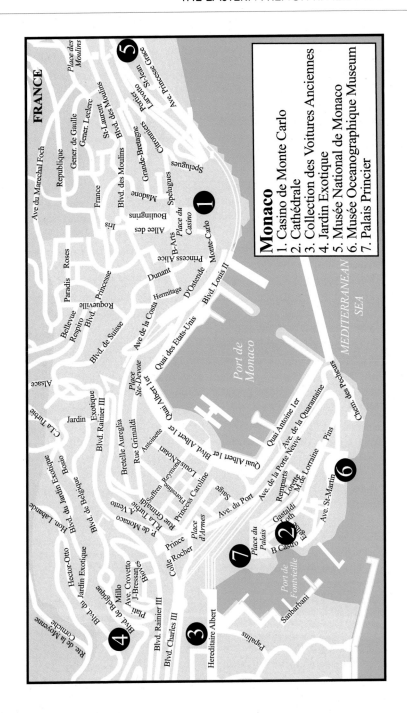

Monaco
1. Casino de Monte Carlo
2. Cathédrale
3. Collection des Voitures Anciennes
4. Jardin Exotique
5. Musée National de Monaco
6. Musée Oceanographique Museum
7. Palais Princier

SIGHTS

6:30pm. Mid-Dec to May Tue-Sun 10:30am-12:30pm and 2pm-5pm. Closed Mon. Oct to mid-Nov daily 10am-5pm. Admission: €4. Combined ticket for Royal Apartments and Museum is €8.

The **Musée Océanographique** (Oceanography Museum), built in 1910, hangs from a cliff in Monaco-Ville. It's sometimes referred to as the Cousteau Aquarium, as Jacques Cousteau, the famous sea-explorer, directed the aquarium until 1988. In addition to its huge (over 90 tanks) and interesting aquarium, the museum contains skeletons of sea creatures (including a giant whale), submarines, and exhibits on the history of sea exploration. Info: avenue St-Martin. Tel. 377/ 93.15.36.00. Open daily Jul and Aug 9:30am-7:30pm, Apr-Jun and Sep 9:30am-7pm, Oct-Mar 10am-6pm. Admission: €13.50, €6 under 18.

You can watch a 35-minute film of the history of Monaco at **The Monte Carlo Story**. Showings are every hour, and you're given headphones for English translation. Info: Terrasses du Parking du Chemin du Pêcheur (next to the Oceanography Museum in the parking garage). Tel. 377/93.25.32.33. Open daily 10am-5pm. Closed Nov and Dec. Admission: €7.

If sitting in a theater is not your style, visit the **Jardin Exotique**. It's an exotic garden with thousands of cacti and succulents. Incredible views of the coast are included in the admission price. Info: boulevard du Jardin Exotique. Tel. 377/93.15.29.80. Open daily mid-May to mid-Sep 9am-7pm (mid-Sep to mid-May until 6pm). Admission: €7.

The **Musée National de Monaco** is located in a luxurious villa (designed by the same man who designed the Casino de Monte Carlo). Surrounded by a rose garden, this special-interest museum houses a collection of dolls and mechanical toys. Info: 17 avenue Princess Grace. Tel. 377/93.30.91.26. Open daily Easter-Sep 10am-6:30pm, Oct-Easter 10am-noon and 2:30pm-6:30pm. Admission: €6.

You could also check out the **Collection des Voitures Anciennes**, the royal collection of over 100 automobiles. Now do they need both a Rolls Royce *and* a Lamborghini? *Info: Les Terrasses de Fontvieille. Tel. 377/92.05.28.56. Open daily 10am-6pm. Admission: €6.*

There's great shopping in Monaco. Main shopping streets include **boulevard des Moulins** (the main street of Monte Carlo), **rue Princess-Caroline** (everything from clothing to baked goods) and **rue Grimaldi** (the main shopping street of the La Condamine area). At **place d'Armes** there is an indoor and outdoor market (every morning).

If you want to shop and feel good about parting with your cash, check out **Boutique du Rocher** with two shops, at 1 avenue de la Madone and 25 rue Emile de Loth. These boutiques were established by Princess Grace to provide an outlet for Monégasque products (everything from linens to dolls). Some products are created at workshops here. The profits all go to the Princess Grace Charitable Foundation.

Monaco really shines in the evening. Head to the incredible **Casino de Monte Carlo**.

Charles Garnier, who designed the opulent Paris Opera House, designed the casino in 1878. Appropriately, there's an opera house inside the casino. The marble atrium with 28 Ionic columns welcomes you (for free). The **Salle Garnier** (named after the architect) is a red-and-gold, opulent concert hall with an 18-ton chandelier. The **Salon Blanc** has painted muses. Perhaps the most interesting room is the **Salon Rose** (the smoking room). Its ceiling is decorated with cigar-smoking female nudes. Roulette is played in both the **Salle Européen**, with its eight gigantic chandeliers, and in the ornate **Renaissance Hall**. The private rooms (**Salles Privées**) are where high rollers gamble surrounded by carved mahogany. The **Salle Américaine** (free admission)

SIGHTS

opens early (at noon) and has Las Vegas-style slot machines. It's without a doubt the world's most glamorous casino. Outside are immaculately maintained gardens, and, in front of the casino, the Art Deco **Café de Paris** where you can sip a pricey mimosa or enjoy a *crêpe Suzette*. *Info: place du Casino. Tel. 377/ 98.06.21.21. Open daily after 2pm. Admission: €10 to the Salle Européen. Additional (at least) €10 to the private backrooms (jacket and tie required in the backrooms. Passport required for entry.)*

You don't have to pay to get into the **Sun Casino** in the Monte Carlo Grand Hotel.

One last sight you have to visit is the **Hôtel de Paris**. Okay, this is a hotel, not a sight. Or is it? Even if you can't afford to stay here or even eat or drink here, you should at least pop in and be dazzled by the magnificent domed entrance. The palatial lobby is a masterpiece of stained glass, statues, crystal chandeliers and marble pillars. It's said that if you rub the raised knee of the bronze statue of Louis XIV's horse in the lobby, you'll have good luck.

The Hill Towns Above Monaco

If you've visited Monaco, you may just want to take it easy in peaceful hill towns. Let's visit a few today. We'll start in **La Turbie**. It's 7 miles (11 km) northeast of Nice (via the Grande Corniche).

There's something very peaceful about La Turbie, located in the hills above the coast. It's not as touristy as nearby Eze, and it certainly is quieter than the coastal towns. The massive Roman monument

La Trophée des Alpes (The Trophy of the Alps) was built in 6 B.C. to celebrate Augustus Caesar's conquest of the Alps. A small museum near the monument, **Musée du Trophée des Alpes**, describes the history of the monument and its restoration. *Info: Tel. 04/ 93.41.20.84, closed Mon, admission: €5.*

After La Turbie, follow the signs to **Peillon**. It's 11 miles (18 km) northeast of Nice.

Peillon is a perched village, but unlike so many of and the

others, it's void of touristy boutiques. Why? It's hard to get to. You may feel like you've stepped back into medieval times. There's only one gateway into this village of ancient homes with red-tiled roofs. You can visit the Baroque church **Eglise St-Saveur** and **Chapelle des Pénitents Blancs**, a chapel with frescoes of the passion of Christ, dating back to the late 15th century.

Though not as unspoiled as Peillon, nearby **Roquebrune** will allow you to wander in relative peace. It's three miles (five km) west of Menton/three miles (five km) east of Monaco.

The perched village of **Roquebrune** is located along the Grande Corniche. The entire village has been renovated, and its steep alleys and arcaded lanes are filled with galleries, boutiques and souvenir shops. The castle on the hilltop is said to be the oldest feudal castle in France, built over 1,000 years ago. You can also visit the 12th-century **Eglise Ste-Marguerite**. The long and narrow street **rue Moncollet** is lined with houses dating back to the Middle Ages. Just outside the village stands

SIGHTS

the **Olivier Millénaire**, a thousand-year-old olive tree, said to be the oldest tree in the world.

The **Château de Roquebrune** is the oldest feudal castle in France. It's dominated by two square towers (with fantastic views of the coast). Inside is a museum tracing the castle's history. *Info: rue du Château. Tel. 04/93.35.07.22. Open daily. Admission: €5.*

Cap-Martin, 1 1/2 miles west of Roquebrune, is a wealthy, mostly residential seaside resort.

Menton
Depending on which way you

look at it, **Menton** is either at the end or the beginning of the French Riviera. It's five miles (nine km) east of Monaco. Menton doesn't feel very French. This isn't solely because of its location on the Italian border, but also a result of the large number of expatriates who have come to Menton to retire. Its climate is the warmest of all the towns in this book, warm enough to grow citrus fruits, and there's a huge **Lemon Festival** (Fête du Citron) held every February. Legend has it that when Adam and Eve were kicked out of the Garden of Eden, Eve snuck out a lemon and planted it in Menton (because the town reminded

her of her former home). There are many lovely gardens in the city. Its long **Promenade du Soleil** (on the **Golfe de la Paix**) runs along a narrow pebble beach and the main costal road. Menton's Old Town, with narrow streets and lively main street **rue St-Michel**, is on the east side of town. It's sedate, but has much to offer the traveler.

There are several museums worth visiting here.

The **Musée des Beaux-Arts** (a fine-arts museum) contains European paintings from the Renaissance to present day. But the real attraction here are the grounds of the **Palais Carnoles**. The gardens of this 18th-century palace (once the summer home of the Princess of Monaco) are filled with orange, grapefruit and lemon trees. *Info: 3 avenue de la Madone (in the Palais Carnoles). Tel. 04/ 93.35.49.71. Closed Tue. Admission: Free.*

The **Musée de Préhistoire Régionale** is dedicated to human evolution. Its highlight is the 30,000-year-old head found in 1884 in nearby caves. *Info: rue Lorédan-*

Larchey. Tel. 04/93.35.84.64. Closed Tue. Admission: Free.

The **Musée Jean-Cocteau** is devoted to the works of writer and artist Jean-Cocteau. It's located in the Bastion du Port, a 17th-century fortress on the port. Cocteau coordinated the restoration of the fortress. *Info: Vieux Port. Info: Tel. 04/ 93.57.72.30. Closed Tue. Admission: €4.*

If you have time, pop into the **Basilique St-Michel**. The bell tower of this Baroque church can be seen throughout Menton. The richly decorated basilica has a huge 17th-century organ. Nearby is the splendid **Chapelle de l'Immaculée-Conception**, dating back to the 1600s. *Info: Parvis St-Michel. Open daily. Admission: Free.*

SIGHTS

In the Old Town between rue St-Michel and the sea is the beautiful **Marché Couvert** (Covered Market). Cheese, fruits, French breads and Italian specialties can all be found here. *Info: Closed Mon.*

Ventimiglia, Italy

Much of the French Riviera was part of Italy until 1860, so you'll see the Italian influence in everything from architecture to cuisine.

Just across the border from Menton is the Italian town of **Ventimiglia** (Vintimille in French). Why not head here for lunch, so when you return from your trip, you can tell friends that you had lunch in Italy? It has a lovely **Città Vecchia** (Old Town), an 11th-century **Duomo** (cathedral), and many restaurants to choose from. Be warned that traffic can be chaotic on Fridays when there's a vast **mercato** (market) selling everything from flowers to leather goods.

Head to the seafront where you'll have your pick of places to eat pasta and seafood.

What a great way to end your week on the Riviera!

BEST SLEEPS & EATS

SLEEPS & EATS

BEAULIEU-SUR-MER
Les Agaves €€-€€€
Attractive and stylish bistro serving regional specialties, especially grilled dishes. Known for their lobster salad. *Info: 4 avenue Maréchal Foch (across from the train station). www.lesagaves.com. Tel. 04/93.01.13.12. Closed mid-Nov to mid-Dec. No lunch.*

EZE
Château Eza €€€
This former residence of Prince William of Sweden is now an elegant hotel built into the medieval walls. Donkeys carry your luggage up the narrow and

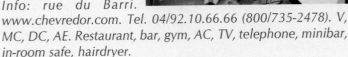

steep cobblestone street. There are only 10 rooms. Extraordinary views. *Info: Rue de la Pise. www.chateaueza.com. Tel. 04/ 93.41.12.24 (800/525-4800). V, MC, DC, AE. Restaurant, bar, AC, TV, telephone, minibar, in-room safe, hairdryer, Internet.*

Hostellerie du Château de la Chèvre d'Or €€€

This incredible luxury-hotel complex of stone houses has 32 rooms. Its secluded setting with narrow alleys has great views of the sea. Truly a unique (and expensive) vacation experience. Its restaurants and outdoor cliffside bar are just the place to splurge. Fabulous infinity pool. *Info: rue du Barri. www.chevredor.com. Tel. 04/92.10.66.66 (800/735-2478). V, MC, DC, AE. Restaurant, bar, gym, AC, TV, telephone, minibar, in-room safe, hairdryer.*

Loumiri €

This bistro near the entry to the old village is a rarity in Eze: It's reasonably priced. Regional dishes are served with affordable local wines. *Info: avenue Jardin Exotique. Tel. 04/93.41.16.42. Closed Mon, Wed (dinner) and mid-Dec to mid-Jan. Inexpensive.*

Restaurant de la Chèvre d'Or €€€

This award-winning restaurant in the Hostellerie du Château de la Chèvre d'Or is one of the best in the French Riviera. The menu features innovative Mediteranean dishes prepared by its star chef. The wine cellar boasts over 20,000 bottles from throughout France. Marble floors, cherry wood panelling, impeccable service, and magnificent panoramic views all add

SLEEPS & EATS

to the experience. *Info:Hostellerie du Château de la Chèvre d'Or.
www.chevredor.com. Reservations required. Tel. 04/92.10.66.60.
Closed Dec to mid-Mar.*

MENTON
La Calanque €€

Italian, Provençal and French food (especially seafood) are
served at this restaurant with harbor views. *Info: 13 square
Victoria. Tel. 04/93.35.83.15. Closed Sun (dinner) and Mon.*

MONACO
Hôtel de Paris €€€

You'll be dazzled by the magnificent domed entrance. The
palatial lobby is a masterpiece
of stained glass, statues, crystal
chandeliers and marble pillars,
and the rooms and service
match the elegance of the common areas. *Info: place du Casino (opposite the casino).
www.montecarloresort.com.
Tel. 377/98.06.30.00. V, MC,
AE. Restaurant, bar, AC, TV, telephone, minibar, in-room safe,
hairdryer, Internet access.*

Hôtel Alexandra €€

Not everyone can afford to stay at the glamorous Hôtel de Paris
or the other exclusive hotels here, and it's not easy to find
affordable hotels in this glitzy place. But, this 56-room hotel in a
charming building in the business district (but not too far from the
casino) provides an ideal alternative. Comfortable and centrally
located. *Info: 35 blvd. Princesse-Charlotte. www.monaco-
hotel.com/montecarlo/alexandra. Tel.377/93.50.63.13. V, MC,
DC, AE. AC, TV, telephone, minibar, hairdryer, wireless Internet.*

Le Louis XV- Alain Ducasse €€€
This restaurant in the luxurious Hôtel de Paris is run by famous
chef Alain Ducasse. Innovative French and Italian cuisine and

attentive service. *Info: place du Casino in the Hôtel de Paris. Tel. 377/98. 06.88.64. Closed Tue and Wed. Open Wed lunch in summer.*

Castelroc €€-€€€
Located across from the palace, this eatery serves local specialties (especially fish). Only fixed-priced meals are available. *Info: place du Palais. Tel. 377/93.30.36.68. Closed Dec through Jan.*

Stars 'n Bars €€
Yearning for a little taste of home? Try this American-style sports bar. *Info: 6 quai Antoine-1er. Tel. 377/97.97.95.95. Closed Mon from Oct-May.*

Pizzeria Monegasque €-€€
Pizza and grilled fish or meat dishes served on the terrace. *Info: 4 rue Terrazzanni. Tel. 377/93.30.16.38. Closed Sun.*

ROQUEBRUNE
Au Grand Inquisiteur €€-€€€
Up a steep stairway on your way to the feudal castle, you'll find

this small restaurant in a cellar. Good Provençal cooking with a huge wine list. Note that sometimes it's closed for lunch. *Info: 18 rue du Château. www.augrandinquisiteur.com. Tel. 04/93.35.05.37. Closed Mon, Tue (lunch), Nov and Dec.*

ST-JEAN-CAP-FERRAT

Grand Hôtel du Cap-Ferrat €€€
Luxurious white palace set in the middle of a 17-acre wooded

estate and subtropical gardens. Its exclusive location is at the tip of the Cap-Ferrat peninsula. Every amenity you can imagine is here. A nice bonus: great views of the sea from its clifftop pool. *Info: St-Jean-Cap-Ferrat. www.grand-hotel-cap-ferrat.com. Tel. 04/93.76.50.50 (800/525-4800). V, MC, DC, AE. Restaurant, bar, outdoor pool, TV, telephone, minibar, hairdryer, safe, Internet.*

Hotel Brise Marine €€
Lovely yellow hotel located in a former villa with a fantastic porch and patio overlooking the water. Great place to unwind. Rooms are comfortable and casual. Highly recommended. *Info: 58 avenue Jean Mermoz. www.hotel-brisemarine.com. Tel. 04/93.76.04.36. V, MC, DC, AE. Bar, TV, telephone, Internet.*

Le Provençal €€€
Fine Provençal dining with a view of the town and the port. Reservations are required, and you must leave room for the famous *"les cinq desserts du Provençal,"* a sampling of five fantastic desserts. *Info: 2 avenue Denis-Séméria. Tel. 04/93.76.03.97. Closed Mon and Tue in winter.*

Le Sloop €€-€€€
You can't miss the blue-and-white décor of this portside restaurant. Fish dishes are featured at the indoor and outdoor tables. *Info: On the port. Tel. 04/93.01.48.63. No lunch Tue and Wed. Closed Wed in winter.*

VILLEFRANCHE-SUR-MER
Hôtel Welcome €€-€€€
This former villa has been renovated into a comfortable hotel. All 36 rooms have balconies with views of the port.

There is a lively restaurant (€€) and wine bar, and it's an excellent location for exploring the town. *Info: 1 quai Amiral-Courbet. www.welcomehotel.com. Tel. 04/93.76.27.62. V, MC, AE. Restaurant, bar, AC, TV, minibar, hairdryer, safe.*

La Mère Germaine €€
Café/restaurant on the waterfront specializing in grilled fish dishes. *Info: quai Courbet. Tel. 04/93.01.71.39. Closed mid-Nov to Dec.*

La Grignotière €€
This friendly restaurant is located near the marketplace and serves local specialties. Delicious pasta dishes. *Info: 3 rue du Poilu. Tel. 04/93.76.79.83. Closed Wed. (except in summer). No lunch.*

Au Clair Obscur €€
You'll find this cozy restaurant at the entry to the interesting rue Obscure, a street covered by vaulted arcades (*photo at right*). Try one of the specialties like *veau au citron* (veal in a citron sauce). *Info: 1 rue Obscure. Tel. 04/93.01.84.88. www.auclairobscur.com. Closed Mon.*

BEST SHOPPING

Menton
In the Old Town between rue St-Michel and the sea is the beautiful **Marché Couvert** (Covered Market), featuring cheese, fruits, French breads and Italian specialties. *Info: Closed Mon.*

SHOPPING

Monaco

At the place d'Armes is an **indoor and outdoor market** (every morning).

Boutique du Rocher

These boutiques were established by Princess Grace to provide an outlet for Monégasque products (everything from linens to dolls), some of which are produced at workshops here. The profits go to the Princess Grace Charitable Foundation. *Info: Two shops, at 1 avenue de la Madone and 25 rue Emile de Loth.*

Ventimiglia, Italy

There's a chaotic *mercato* (**market**) on Fridays selling everything from flowers to leather goods.

Villefranche-sur-Mer

There's a **market** on Sundays at place Amélie Pollonais.

BEST NIGHTLIFE & ENTERTAINMENT

NIGHTLIFE & ENTERTAINMENT

Eze

Hostellerie du Château de la Chèvre d'Or

Have a drink at sunset at the outdoor cliffside hotel bar (*photo below*). But be warned – there's a steep minimum drink order on weekends. *Info: rue du Barri. Tel. 04/92.10.66.66. Closed mid-Nov to Feb.*

Monaco Happenings

The **Spring Arts Festival** (Printemps des Arts) featuring symphonic, opera and ballet performances is held each April to mid-May. The **Monte Carlo Tennis Tournament** is held at the same time. Two major auto races are held in Monaco: The famous **Grand Prix de Monaco** takes place in mid-May, and **Le Rallye** take place in January. Each June, Monte Carlo hosts the **International Festival of Television** (Le Festival International de la Télévision), the television version of the Cannes Film Festival.

12. PRACTICAL MATTERS

GETTING TO THE SOUTH OF FRANCE
Airports/Arrival

The **Nice-Côte d'Azur Airport** is located on a peninsula between Nice and Antibes. It's 20 minutes west of the central city of Nice. A taxi into town costs at least €35. Buses run at least every 30 minutes to the central city to both the SNCF train station and the municipal bus station (Gare Routière) for less than €4 (buses 23, 98 and 99). Check with the helpful staff at the airport bus station in Terminal 1. Once in Nice, hop on the new tram to get around town (€1 single ride, €4 day pass).

The **Marseille Airport** (located in Marignane) is 17 miles northwest of the city. Minivans (called *navettes*) leave for Marseille's St-Charles rail station every 20 minutes, 6am-10pm, for €9.

All major car-rental companies are represented at both airports.

You can also fly to Paris and then take a train south (*see next page*).

GETTING AROUND
Cars & Driving

Renting a car and driving is the best way to see the areas covered in this book. Note that parking can be difficult in high season. Driving within major cities (Nice, Marseille and Avignon) can be a headache. Gas is very expensive, but a mitigating factor is that the cars are smaller and more energy-efficient. You will either take a ticket when you get on the autoroute and pay (look for the signs that say *péage*) when you get off, or pay as you go.

In order of fastest to slowest, routes are as follows: A means **autoroute**, N means **national route**, and D means **departmental route**. Be prepared for narrow roads, high speeds and hairpin turns.

Train & Bus Travel

SNCF is the rail system for France. **TGV** trains are fast-speed trains that travel at up to 220 mph. TGV trains **departing from Paris's Charles-de-Gaulle Airport** serve:

- **Aix-en-Provence**, 3 hours
- **Arles**, 4 hours
- **Avignon**, 2 hours and 40 minutes
- **Cannes**, 6 hours via Marseille
- **Nîmes**, 3 hours
- **Marseille**, 3 hours and 15 minutes
- **Orange**, 3 hours

Aix-en-Provence and Avignon have TGV stations on the edge of town. The trip on the TGV **from Paris to Nice** is 6 hours, as not all of the trip is high-speed. *Info: www.sncf.com.*

There's a **coastal rail line** that runs from Ventimiglia on the Italian border (Vintimille in French) to Marseille. There are trains that run nearly every hour on this line. Stops on this scenic train ride include: Menton, Cap-Martin, Monaco, Èze-sur-Mer (not to be confused with hilltop Èze), Beaulieu, St-Jean-Cap-Ferrat, Villefranche-sur-Mer, Nice, Antibes and Cannes. Local trains serve many Provence and Riviera towns. You must validate (*composter*) your ticket at a machine (watch locals do it) before you get on a SNCF train.

Regional bus service is good, but is limited on Sundays. Train service is in most cases faster, but bus service is generally cheaper.

FESTIVALS

January
- Monte Carlo Motor Rally (Le Rallye) in Monte Carlo

February
- Lemon Festival (Fête du Citron) in Menton

February-March (Easter)
- Carnival in Nice
- Easter Bullfighting Festival (Féria Pascale) in Arles
- Procession of the Dead Christ (Procession du Christ Mort), a religious procession, in Roquebrune-Cap Martin
- Procession of the Penitents (Procession des Pénitents), religious processions in Collioure and Arles

April

- The Spring Arts Festival (Printemps des Arts), featuring symphonic, opera and ballet performances, held April to mid-May in Monte Carlo
- The Monte Carlo Tennis Tournament, held April to mid-May in Monte Carlo
- Olympic Sailing Week, a sailing competition featuring 1,000 boats from over 50 nations, in Hyères

May

- Festival des Musiques d'Aujour d'hui, a musical festival featuring young artists, in Marseille
- Festival of the Move to Summer Grazing (Fête de la Transhumance), a sheep drive to upland summer pastures, in St-Rémy. The entire town is loaded with sheep and goats in mid- to late May
- Cowboy Festival (La Fête des Gardians), a festival celebrating the cowboys from the Camargue, in Arles
- Gypsies' Pilgrimage (Le Pélerinage des Gitans), a gathering of Gypsies as part of a religious pilgrimage, in Stes-Maries-de-la-Mer
- International Film Festival (Festival International du Film) in Cannes

- Grand Prix de Monaco, auto race in mid-May, in Monte Carlo

June

- Festival de Marseille Méditerranée, Mediterranean music festival in late June and early July, in Marseille
- Classical music festival (Festival Aix en Musique) in Aix-en-Provence
- Fête de la Tarasque, a festival celebrating the legend of Tarasque (a dragon-like beast) being subdued by Saint Martha, in Tarascon
- Reconstitution Historique, a festival honoring Nostradamus, in Salon-de-Provence

July

- Bastille Day, celebrating the fall of the Bastille Prison, on July 14. Celebrations throughout the region
- Fishermen's Festival (La Fête des Pêcheurs) in early July in Cassis
- Festival d'Aix, classical street performance, in Aix-en-Provence
- Beach Volleyball World Series in Marseille
- Musical festival (Nuits Musicales d'Uzès), last two weeks of July, in Uzès
- Festival of dance, theatre and music (Festival d'Avignon),

the last three weeks of July and the first week of August, in Avignon

- Opera and classical music fair (Les Chorégies d'Orange) in Orange
- Musical and theatrical events (Festival Lacoste) in Lacoste (July and August)
- Jazz Festival, end of July, in Aix-en-Provence
- Jazz Festival in Juan-les-Pins
- Jazz Festival in Nice
- Nikaia, international athletics event, in Nice
- Pétanque Championships, (also known as *boules*), in Marseille
- Nightime Bull Festival (Nuit Taurine), the French version of Pamplona's "Running of the Bulls," in mid-July in St-Rémy

August
- Wine Festival (Fête de la Véraison), first weekend, in Châteauneuf-du-Pape
- Fêtes Daudet, a folk festival, in Fontvieille
- Féria de St-Rémy, a bull festival (including bull fights with matadors on horseback), in St-Rémy

September
- Rice Harvest Festival (Féria des Prémices du Riz), a regional festival including bullfights, in Arles

- Festival of Olives (Journée de l"Olivier), festival of the olive, in late-September in Salon-de-Provence

October
- Gypsies' Pilgrimage (Le Pélerinage des Gitans), a gathering of Gypsies as part of a religious pilgrimage, in Stes-Maries-de-la-Mer
- String Quartet Festival (Musique en Pays) late October and early November, in Fayence

November
- *Santons* Festival (Marché aux Santons), craft festival featuring *santons* (terra-cotta figurines), in Tarascon

December
- Christmas Fair (Foire de Noël), Christmas gift and ornament fair, in Mougins
- Provence Christmas (Noël Provençal), traditional procession of shepherds followed by Midnight Mass on Christmas Eve, in Les Baux
- *Santons* Fair (Foire aux Santons), craft festival featuring *santons* (terra-cotta figurines), in Marseille
- New Year's Eve (Fête de St-Sylvestre), everyone heads outdoors to the old town centers to celebrate

HOLIDAYS
- New Year's: January 1
- Easter
- Ascension (40 days after Easter)
- Pentecost (seventh Sunday after Easter)
- May Day: May 1
- Victory in Europe: May 8
- Bastille Day: July 14
- Assumption of the Virgin Mary: August 15
- All Saints': November 1
- Armistice: November 11
- Christmas: December 25

BASIC INFORMATION
Banking & Changing Money
The **euro** (€) is the currency of France and most of Europe. Before you leave for France, it's a good idea to get some euros. It makes your arrival a lot easier. Call your credit-card company or bank before you leave to tell them that you'll be using your ATM or credit card outside the country. Many have automatic controls that can "freeze" your account if the computer program determines that there are charges outside your normal area.

ATMs (with fees, of course) are the easiest way to change money in France. You'll find them everywhere. You can still get traveler's checks, but why bother?

Kilometers-Miles
One kilometer = 0.62 miles. To convert miles to kilometers, multiply by 1.61. So, 1 mile = 1.61 kilometers.

Business Hours
Many attractions and offices in Provence close at noon and re-open and hour or two later.

Climate & Weather
Expect hot and dry weather except for periods of heavy rain in spring. November, December and January can be quite cold and wet, with temperatures dipping to lows in the upper 30s. The average high temperature in July and August is 84 degrees. The Mistral wind blows 30 to 60 miles per hour about 100 days of the year in Provence. It begins above the Alps and Massif Central Mountains, gaining speed as it heads south toward

Consulates & Embassies
- **US Consulate, Nice**: *7 avenue Gustave V, Tel. 04/ 93.88.89.55*
- **US Consulate, Marseille**: *place Varian-Fry, Tel. 04/ 91.54.92.00*
- **Canadian Consulate, Nice**: *2 place Franklin, Tel. 04/ 93.92.93.22*

Electricity

The electrical current in France is **220 volts** as opposed to 110 volts found at home. Don't fry your electric razor, hairdryer or laptop. You'll need a converter and an adapter. Some laptops don't require a converter, but why are you bringing them on vacation anyway?

Emergencies & Safety

Don't wear a fanny pack; it's a sign that you're a tourist and an easy target (especially in crowded tourist areas). Avoid wearing expensive jewelry. Don't leave valuables in your car. **In case of an emergency, dial 17 for the police, 15 for an ambulance and 18 for the fire department**. Pharmacies can refer you to a doctor.

Insurance

Check with your health-care provider. Most policies don't cover you overseas. If that's the case, you may want to obtain medical insurance. Given the uncertainties in today's world, you may also want to purchase **trip-cancellation insurance**. Make sure that your policy covers sickness, disasters, bankruptcy and State Department travel restrictions and warnings. In other words, read the fine print! *Info: www.insuremytrip.com for insurance coverage.*

Internet Access

Cyber cafés seem to pop up everywhere (and go out of business quickly). You shouldn't have difficulty finding a place to e-mail home. Remember that French keyboards are different than those found in the U.S. and Canada. The going rate is about 2€ per hour.

Language

Please, make the effort to speak a little French. It will get you a long way, even if all you can say is *Parlez-vous anglais?* (par-lay voo ahn-glay): Do you speak English? Gone are the days when the French were only interested in correcting your French. There's a list of helpful French phrases in this book.

Packing

Never pack prescription drugs, eyeglasses or valuables. Carry them on. Think black. It always works for men and women. Oh, and by the way, pack light. Don't ruin your trip by having to lug around huge suitcases. Before you leave home, make copies of your passport, airline tickets and confirmation of hotel reservations. You should also make a list of your credit-card numbers and the telephone numbers for your credit-card companies. If you lose any of them (or they're stolen), you can call someone at home and have them provide the information to you. You should also pack copies of these documents separate from the originals.

Passport Regulations

You'll need a **valid passport** to enter France. If you're staying more than 90 days, you must obtain a visa. Canadians don't need visas. Canadians can bring back C$750 each year if they have been gone for 7 days or more.

US citizens who have been away more than 48 hours can bring home $800 of merchandise duty-free every 30 days. *Info: go to Traveler Information (Know Before You Go) at www.customs.gov.*

Postal Services

Post offices – **PTT** – are found in nearly every town. You'll recognize them by their yellow *La Poste* signs. They're generally open weekdays from 8am-7pm and Saturdays from 8am until noon. Some post offices, especially those in smaller towns, close for an hour or two in the middle of the day.

Rest Rooms

There aren't a lot of public rest rooms. If you need to go, your best bet is to head (no pun intended) to the nearest café or *brasserie*. It's considered good manners to purchase something if you use the rest room. Don't be shocked to walk into a rest room and find two porcelain footprints and a hole in the floor. These old "Turkish toilets" still exist. Hope you have strong thighs!

Taxes

Hotel and restaurant prices are required by law to include taxes and service charges. **Value Added Tax** (VAT or TVA in France) is nearly 20% (higher on luxury goods). The VAT is included in the price of goods (except services such as restaurants). Foreigners are entitled to a refund and must fill out a refund form. When you make your purchase, you should ask for the form and instructions if you're purchasing €175 or more in one place and in one day (no combining). Yes, it can be a hassle. *Info: Check out www.globalrefund.com for the latest information on refunds (and help for a fee).*

Telephone

- Country code for France is **33**
- Area code for Provence and the French Riviera is **04**
- Calls beginning with 0800 are toll-free
- Calling France from the U.S. and Canada: dial 011-33-4 plus the eight-digit local

number. You drop the 0 in the area code
- Calling the U.S. or Canada from Paris: dial 00 (wait for the tone), dial 1 plus the area code and local number
- Calling within Provence and the French Riviera: dial 04 and the eight-digit local number.

Phone cards are the cheapest way to call. Get one from many *tabacs*, métro stations or magazine kiosks.

A great way to stay in touch and save money is to **rent an international cell phone**. One provider is www.cellhire.com. Few cell phones purchased in the U.S. work in Europe. If you're a frequent visitor to Europe, you may want to purchase a cell phone (for about $50) from www.mobal.com. You'll get an international telephone number, and pay for calls by the minute.

Time
When it's noon in New York City, it's 6pm in Provence. For hours of events or schedules, the French use the 24-hour clock. So 6am is 06h00 and 1pm is 13h00.

Tipping
See the restaurant section, beginning on page 201, for tipping in restaurants. Other tips: 10%

for taxi drivers, €1 for room service, €1.50 per bag to the hotel porter, €1.50 per day for maid service and €0.50 to bathroom attendants.

Tourist Information
Nearly every town in this book has a helpful tourist-information center. Tourist offices in Avignon and Arles sell money-saving museum passes. Many museums in Nice now have free entry.

Water
Tap water is safe in France. Occasionally, you'll find *non potable* signs in rest rooms. This means that the water is not safe for drinking.

Web Sites
For the **French Government Tourist Office** go to www.franceguide.com. For the **US State Department Foreign Entry Requirements** go to www.state.gov.

HOTELS & RESTAURANTS
Hotels
I've listed hotels throughout Provence and the French Riviera in this book. I've also included some wonderful bed-and-breakfast establishments and farmhouses that have been converted into inns and hotels.

In addition to the lodgings in this chapter, you could also stay at

Hotel Prices in this Book

Prices for two people in a double room:

- **Expensive** (over €200): €€€
- **Moderate** (€100-200): €€
- **Inexpensive** (under €100): €

one of the many *gîtes* (country homes that can be rented by travelers, usually by the week). In an effort to preserve these country homes, the French government offers subsidies to rehabilitate them and a program to market them for rental. There are thousands of these homes in France, from luxury to budget. For information on this great way to experience France, especially if traveling as a family or group, visit *www.gite.com* or *www.gites-de-france.fr/eng.*

Restaurants

You've come to France in part to enjoy the best cuisine in the world, right? You will not be disappointed. I have selected the best restaurants within different price ranges, and I also give you some tips beginning on the next page to help you save money and still eat a meal that will be memorable and *fantastique* in every way!

There's no need to spend a lot of money in Provence and the French Riviera to eat well. Of course it hurts when the dollar is weaker than the euro, but there are all kinds of fabulous foods to be had inexpensively.

Eat at a neighborhood restaurant or bistro. You'll always know the price of a meal before entering, as almost all restaurants post the menu and prices in the window. Never order anything whose price is not known in advance. If you see *selon grosseur* (sometimes abbreviated as *s/g*) this means that you're paying by weight, which can be extremely expensive.

Delis and food stores can provide cheap and wonderful meals. Buy some cheese, bread, wine and other snacks and have a picnic. In fact, no matter what, you should go into a *boulangerie*

Restaurant Prices in this Book

Restaurant prices in this book are for a main course and without wine:

- **Expensive:** (over €20) €€€
- **Moderate:** (€10-20) €€
- **Inexpensive:** (under €10) €

Eating & Drinking Advice

The author of this book is the author of *Eating & Drinking in Paris*. This pocket book has an extensive menu translator to help you decipher menus all over France. You can order it from amazon.com or *www.openroadguides.com*.

and buy a *baguette* at least once. Remember to pack a corkscrew and eating utensils when you leave home.

Lunch, even at the most expensive restaurants listed in this guide, always has a lower fixed price. So have lunch as your main meal. Many French do.

Restaurants and bistros that have menus written in English (especially those near tourist attractions) are almost always more expensive than neighborhood restaurants and bistros.

Street vendors in larger towns generally sell inexpensive and terrific food; you'll find excellent hot dogs, crêpes and roast-chicken sandwiches.

For the cost of a cup of coffee or a drink, you can linger at a café and watch the world pass you by for as long as you want. It's one of France's greatest bargains.

The **bill** in a restaurant is called *l'addition* ... but the bill in a bar is called *le compte* or *la note*. Confused? It's easier if you just make a scribbling motion with your fingers on the palm of your hand.

A **service charge** is almost always added to your bill. Depending on the service, it's sometimes appropriate to leave an additional 5 to 10%. The menu will usually note that service is included (*service compris*). Sometimes this is abbreviated with the letters s.c. The letters s.n.c. stand for *service non compris*; this means that the service is not included in the price, and you must leave a tip. You'll sometimes find *couvert* or cover charge on your menu (a small charge just for placing your butt at the table).

A *menu* is a fixed-price meal, not that piece of paper listing the food items. If you want **what we consider a menu**, you need to ask for *la carte*. The menu is almost always posted on the front of the restaurant so you know what you're getting into, both foodwise and pricewise, before you enter.

Mealtimes

Lunch is served from around 1pm and dinner from around 9pm. Make reservations!

Dogs Allowed!

The French really love their dogs. In restaurants, it's not uncommon to find several dogs under tables, or even on their own chairs.

ESSENTIAL PHRASES

please, *s'il vous plait* (seel voo *play*)

thank you, *merci* (*mair* see)

yes, *oui* (wee)

no, *non* (nohn)

good morning, *bonjour* (bohn *jhoor*)

good afternoon, *bonjour* (bohn *jhoor*)

good evening, *bonsoir* (bohn *swahr*)

goodbye, *au revoir* (o ruh *vwahr*)

sorry/excuse me, *pardon* (pahr-dohn)

You are welcome, *de rien* (duh ree *ehn*)

Do you speak English?, *parlez-vous anglais?* (par lay voo ahn *glay*)

I don't speak French, *je ne parle pas français* (jhuh ne parl pah frahn *say*)

I don't understand, *je ne comprends pas* (jhuh ne kohm *prahn* pas)

I'd like a table, *je voudrais une table* (zhuh voo *dray* ewn tabl)

I'd like to reserve a table, *je voudrais réserver une table* (zhuh voo *dray* rayzehrvay ewn tabl)

for one, *pour un* (poor oon), two, *deux* (duh), *trois* (twah)(3) , *quatre* (*kaht*-ruh)(4), *cinq* (sank)(5), *six* (cease)(6), *sept* (set)(7), *huit* (wheat)(8), *neuf* (nerf)(9), *dix* (dease)(10)

waiter/sir, *monsieur* (muh-*syuh*) – note: never *garçon*!

waitress/miss, *mademoiselle* (mad mwa *zel*)

knife, *couteau* (koo *toe*)

spoon, *cuillère* (kwee *air*)

fork, *fourchette* (four *shet*)

menu, *la carte* (la cart) (not *menu*!)

wine list, *la carte des vins* (la cart day van)

no smoking, *défense de fumer* (day *fahns* de fu may)

toilets, *les toilettes* (lay twa *lets*)

closed, *fermé* (fehr-may)

open, *ouvert* (oo-vehr)

today, *aujourd'hui* (o zhoor dwee)

tomorrow, *demain* (duh *mehn*)

tonight, *ce soir* (suh *swahr*)

Monday, *lundi* (luhn dee)

Tuesday, *mardi* (mahr dee)

Wednesday, *mercredi* (mair kruh dee)

Thursday, *jeudi* (jheu *dee*)
Friday, *vendredi* (vawn druh *dee*)
Saturday, *samedi* (sahm *dee*)
Sunday, *dimanche* (dee mahnsh)

here, *ici* (ee-*see*)
there, *là* (la)
what, *quoi* (kwah)
when, *quand* (kahn)
where, *où est* (ooh-eh)
how much, *c'est combien* (say comb bee *ehn*)
credit cards, *les cartes de crédit* (lay kart duh creh *dee*)

KNOW WHAT YOU'RE ORDERING!
Provence Food & Drink Specialties
aïoli/ailloli, garlic mayonnaise
anchoïade, anchovy spread
banon, cheese dipped in eau-de-vie and wrapped in chestnut leaves
boeuf à la gordienne, braised beef dish
cachat, fresh cheese
cavaillon, a fragrant melon from the town of the same name. It looks like a small cantaloupe
champignon de pin, pine mushroom (a wild mushroom)
daube provençal, gravy with capers, garlic and anchovies
escabèche, raw fish marinated in lime juice and herbs/a cold marinated sardine dish
estouffados, almond butter cookies

farigoule or **frigolet**, wild thyme
fromage fort, extremely soft cheese mixed with herbs, salt, pepper and *marc*
herbes de Provence, mixture of herbs that includes fennel, lavender, marjoram, bay leaf, sage, rosemary and thyme
lapin en paquets, rabbit pieces in a packet of bacon
lavande, lavender. Lavender blossoms are added to dishes such as *sorbet de lavande* (lavender sorbet)
lou maïs, corn-meal cake
marc, a strong liqueur made from distilling the residue of grapes (similar to Italian grappa)
muge, mullet
parme, amberjack
pastis, anise-flavored aperitif. This is a Provençal word meaning mixture. It's a summer drink. Common brands are Pastis 51, Pernod, Ricard, Granier, Prado and Henri Bardouin
petits farcis provençaux, stuffed vegetables
picodon, goat's-milk cheese
pissaladière, pizza-like tart with onions, black olives and purée of anchovies and sardines
provençale, à la, with garlic, onions, herbs and tomatoes ("Provence style")

quartiers d'orange glacés, caramelized orange sections
tapenade, mixture of black olives, olive oil, lemon juice, capers and anchovies (a spread)
tian de Saint-Jacques et légumes provençal, sea scallops on a bed of chopped vegetables
tomates à la provençal, baked tomatoes stuffed with bread crumbs, garlic and parsley
trouchia, an omelet (in most of France, this means trout)
violet de Provence, braid of garlic

pissaladière, pizza-like tart with onions, black olives and purée of anchovies and sardines
ratatouille, eggplant casserole
salade niçoise, salad usually with tomatoes, anchovies or tuna, potatoes, vinegar and black olives
socca, crêpe made with chickpea flour
stockfish, spicy fish stew

You'll also find such Italian pasta favorites as **gnocchi** and **ravioli** on many menus.

Nice/French Riviera Food & Drink Specialties

bohémienne, eggplant and tomato casserole
daube à la niçoise, beef or lamb stew with red wine, tomatoes and onions
farci, a dish of stuffed vegetables
lou pevre, goat's-milk cheese with coarsely ground pepper
lou piech, stuffed veal dish
niçoise, usually means with tomatoes, anchovies, vinegar and black olives
pan bagnat, large round sandwich filled with olive oil, onions, olives, tomatoes, anchovies and a hard-boiled egg. A specialty on the Côte d'Azur (means "wet bread"). This is a *salade niçoise* sandwich

INDEX

Things Change!

Phone numbers, prices, addresses, quality of service – all change. If you come across any new information, let us know. No item is too small! Contact us at :

jopenroad@aol.com
or
www.openroadguides.com

PHOTO CREDITS

The following photos are from wikimedia commons: p. 15 bottom: Jialiang Gao; pp. 10, 24: Marc Ryckaert; p. 31 top left: Pierre-Emmanuel Malissin et Frederic Valdes; p. 37: Chimigi; p. 62: Vi..Cult...; p. 99: Joel Takv; pp. 109, 115: Baptiste Rossi; p. 124: N. Baxter; p. 131: Markus Bernet; p. 139 top: Otto Normalverbraucher; p. 142: rdavout; p. 158: jmreymond; p. 160: mgO2; p. 183 left: Ophelie A.

The following photo is from Jan Tyler: pp. 1, 40: *The following photo is from Chin-Kiu Chris Cheng*: p. 11 bottom. *The following photo is from Jean-Paul Mission*: p. 155.

The following images are from flickr.com: p. 9 : nicephore; p. 11 top: zeerood; p. 16 bottom: rKistian; p. 17: hsivonen; p. 22: skycaptaintwo; pp. 23, : Andy Hay; p. 26: lorentey; pp. 27, : wyzik; p. 31 top: m-louis; pp. 14 bottom, 17, 31 left and bottom, 82, 92: Wolfgang Staudt; pp. 15 top, 33, 44, 52, 107: jean-louis zimmermann; pp. 35 bottom, 47, 58, 89 left: Allie Caulfield; pp. 36, 87: http2007; p. 39: Bronx Teacher; p. 42: prozacblues; pp. 43, : Lance and Erin; p. 46: TracyElaine; p. 53: jasonb42882; p. 55 bottom: Fabrice Terrasson; p. 56 left: woodleywonderworks; p. 56 right: jez.atkinson; pp. 3 bottom, 16 top, 57, 93 top: Aschaf; pp. 3 top, 8, 14 top, 59, 83, 91 top, 171, 213 (both), 214 bottom photos: myhsu; p. 60: Petteri Sulonen; p. 61: jatdoll; p. 68: georgeoscarlbluth; p. 69: anjci; p. 71: MartinDube; p. 72: stephanemartin; p. 75: ho visto nina volare; p. 80: luvpreloved; p. 81: Ben Bowes; p. 86: Gael Chardon; p. 89 right: Peter Curbishley; p. 90: RachScottHalls; p. 91 bottom: Claudia Castro; p. 93 bottom: Steve Parker; p. 101: papalars; p. 106 top: austinevan; p. 106 bottom: mcveja; pp. 108: benoit.darcy; p. 110: bibendum84; p. 111: Roxanne Peck; p. 116, 214 top: Michael Gwyther-Jones; p. 118: ExperienceLA; p. 121: 4StringsGood; p. 123: ShelleyC28; p. 125: TravelEden; p. 129: Mr Dotcom; p. 132: m-louis; p. 133: Cameron Nordholm; p. 134: Kevin Lawver; p. 137: Sherrif of Nothing; p. 139 bottom: tiseb; p. 140: John Mahowald; p. 143 bottom: Stephen Shingler; p. 144: Eric Borda; p. 151: FaceMePLS; p. 153: Jeremy Couture; p. 157: a.drian; p. 159: reenie; p. 162: Rosino; p. 166: menzoo; p. 169: Jon Mountjoy; p. 170: maxf; p. 172: travel-junkie; p. 173: genvessel; p. 174 left: Damian Morys Foto; p. 174 right: hillsieboy; p. exfordyswife; p. 176: wit; p. 177: adomass; p. 178: manitou2121; p. 181: tylerdurden1; p. 183 right: alexbrn; p. 184: Suomi Star; p. 185: kirandulo; p. 188: P'con; p. 191 (both photos): CharlotteKinzie; p. 193: jeffwilcox; p. 194: copelaes; pp. 203: Leonard Vaughan (www.flickr.com/photos/cordsimages).

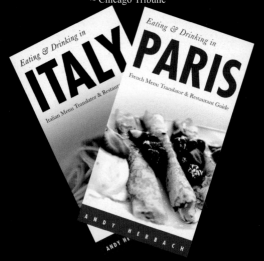